SEAFOOD RECIPES

A Seafood Cookbook With Delicious Seafood Recipes

(A New Seafood Cookbook Filled With Delicious Seafood Recipes)

Kenneth Gable

Published by Alex Howard

© Kenneth Gable

All Rights Reserved

Seafood Recipes: A Seafood Cookbook With Delicious Seafood Recipes (A New Seafood Cookbook Filled With Delicious Seafood Recipes)

ISBN 978-1-990169-83-0

All rights reserved. No part of this guide may be reproduced in any form without permission in writing from the publisher except in the case of brief quotations embodied in critical articles or reviews.

Legal & Disclaimer

The information contained in this book is not designed to replace or take the place of any form of medicine or professional medical advice. The information in this book has been provided for educational and entertainment purposes only.

The information contained in this book has been compiled from sources deemed reliable, and it is accurate to the best of the Author's knowledge; however, the Author cannot guarantee its accuracy and validity and cannot be held liable for any errors or omissions. Changes are periodically made to this book. You must consult your doctor or get professional medical advice before using any of the suggested remedies, techniques, or information in this book.

Table of contents

Part 1 1

Introduction 2

Basic Cooking Techniques 8

Terms & Abbreviations 12

Buttered Prawns With Egg Floss 13

Drunken Prawns 15

Fried Prawns In Tamarind Juice 17

Stir Fried Clams with Green Mango 19

Prawns in Butter and Cheese Sauce 22

Steamed Squid with Spicy Bean Sauce 24

Grilled Squid 25

Spicy Fish Stew With Bean Sauce 27

Steamed Fried Fish Rolls with Asparagus 29

Steamed Prawns With Ginger 31

Stir Fried Prawns with Sweet Plum Sauce 32

Pan Fried Red Snapper with Tamarind Sauce 33

Crispy Coconut Prawns 34

Steamed Cod Fish With Mushroom	36
Nourishing Herbal Steamed Fish	37
Prawns and Vegetables Salad	39
Stir Fried Cuttlefish	40
King Prawns in Hoisin Sauce With Sesame Seed	41
Deep Fried Black Pomfret in Tangy Sauce	43
Deep Fried Honey Sesame Prawns	44
Stir Fried Abalone With Broccoli	46
Savoury Sardines In Tomato Sauce	47
Braised Crab in Clay Pot	48
Fried Crab In Black Pepper Sauce	51
Deep Fried Stuffed Squid	53
Steamed Halibut With Szechuan Cabbage	55
Fish Fillet with Tangy Orange Sauce	57
Thai Style Steamed Fish	59
Prawn Bean Curd Stew In Clay Pot	61
Tamarind Stingray Curry	63
Fried Red Snapper In Sauce	65

Super Stuffed Crab Meat Mushrooms	67
Fast And Furious Shrimp	69
Island Soul Seafood Stew	70
Hawaiian Mushrooms Stuffed with Crab	72
Belgian Endive Stuffed with Crabmeat Ravigote	73
Steam Red Pepper Shellfish (Mussels)	75
Mussels Vinaigrette	78
Thai-Style Mussels with Pickled Ginger	80
Broiled Mussels with Sweet Paprika Aioli	82
Avocado and Shrimp Rafts	84
Shrimp-Stuffed Avocados	85
Shrimp Stuffed Avocados	87
Shrimp Stuffed Grape Leaves	89
Prawn Cocktail	92
Lucious Lime Shrimp	94
Low-Carb Coconut Shrimp	96
Gluten Free Coconut Shrimp	98
Coconut Shrimp	99

Low Carb Coconut Battered Shrimp 101

Baked Coconut Shrimp 103

Broiled Marinated Shrimp 105

Shrimp Mojo de Ajo 107

Sesame Shrimp with Cilantro-Lime Sauce 108

Cilantro Pesto Shrimp 110

Barbecued Calamari 112

Grilled Calamari 114

Roasted Red Pepper, Garlic and Anchovy Appetizer 116

Black Olive Tapenade 117

Green Olive Tapenade 119

Olive Tapenade 120

Black Olive Paste 121

Olive-Caper Spread 122

Salsa Verde 123

Smoked Salmon with Mango and Coconut 124

Roasted Asparagus Wrapped in Smoked Salmon 125

Asparagus and Smoked Salmon Bundles 126

Smoked Salmon Wrapped Scallops With Pistachio Horseradish Crust 128

Shrimp Salmon Rumaki with Dill Mayonnaise 130

Smoked Salmon with Mango and Coconut 131

Roasted Asparagus Wrapped in Smoked Salmon 132

Asparagus and Smoked Salmon Bundles 133

Smoked Salmon Wrapped Scallops With Pistachio Horseradish Crust 135

Shrimp Salmon Rumaki with Dill Mayonnaise 138

Tuna Salad Bites 139

Tuna Tartare 141

Asian Tuna Tartare 142

Tuna Tartare Sicilian-Style 144

Conclusion 146

Part 2 147

CEDAR KEY CRAB BISQUE 148

EL DORA CRAB CAKES 152

J.B.'S FISH CAMP 1960s–2008 154

NEW SYMRNA BEACH   CRAB IMPERIAL 156

SAVANNAH SHE-CRAB SOUP 160

GRILLED YELLOWTAIL SNAPPER 164

FISHING THE F.I.T.O.A. 166

MAHI-MAHI FITOA STYLE 168

RED SNAPPER FISHING: 1803–2008 169

LEMON STUFFED FISH 172

TARPON SPRINGS 1961 174

TAMPA BAY FILET 176

BACK BAY SAUTE' 180

CLEARWATER GROUPER SUPREME 182

TAMPA SWEET PEPPER PASTRY 186

HERNANDO COBIA VERMOUTH 190

Part 1

Introduction

I believe that anyone can cook. It is extremely easy to prepare a meal the Chinese way. Chinese cooking is healthy and fast. It does not consist of a lot of oil or fat. For example, stir frying is great for cooking vegetables as the quick cooking process prevents loss of nutrients. In fact, if you are tired of eating steamed vegetables for health reason, try stir fry. It gives you a whole new way of enjoying your vegetables. Chinese cooking is truly great if you are trying to lose weight or want to lead a healthier lifestyle.

If you have eaten Chinese food in the restaurant or take away, you will notice that most Chinese food is laden with MSG (Mono-sodium Glutamate) to enhance the flavors. I do not agree with using any food additives or enhancers as what we should enjoy is the authentic and natural taste of the food. You will find that my recipes use only natural ingredients. Feel free to experiment with the recipes. If you feel that you like stronger taste, do add more sea salt or natural seasonings. Chinese recipes are quite flexible. You will not ruin a meal if you make a little change to suit your taste buds.

If you are familiar with Chinese cooking, please proceed to the recipes. However, if you are new to Chinese cooking, I am going to briefly describe the basic equipment, ingredients and techniques which you need to know before you start cooking. I hope you enjoy the book and inspires you to start cooking!

Cooking Utensils

In Chinese cooking, what you really need is only a good knife or two and a wok. Woks come in all shapes and sizes, but I still prefer my old carbon steel wok with it's rounded bottom and one wooden handle. Do you know the older the wok is, the tastier is the food? An old wok just gives a unique 'wok' flavor to the food.

Before you are ready to cook with a wok, you need to season it. How to season a wok? First, you need to scrub it with a mild cream cleanser to remove any residue and dry it carefully. Put the wok on the stove over low flame. Coat the inside of the wok with two tablespoons of cooking oil using a kitchen towel.

Let the wok heat up slowly for 10 to 15 minutes, then wipe the wok with more kitchen towel. The paper will come away black. Carry on coating, heating and cleaning until the kitchen towel comes away clean. Your wok is now ready to use. After use, wash only in water without detergent and dry thoroughly over low heat. You may also apply a little oil if you wish. This should prevent the wok from rusting but if it does develop rust, just scrub it and season again.

However, if this sounds too much work, you can buy non stick woks which are very common these days.

Basic Ingredients

Chinese cooking involves simple ingredients. For basic cooking, common essential ingredients include, ginger, garlic and onion. These are used as a base for just any type of Chinese cooking, especially stir frying. To save time, you can actually use a food processor to mince more garlic, add a little oil in it and store it in a glass jar. Garlic can be kept quite well this way, it should last up to 2 weeks. Whenever, you need it, just take what you need and store the rest back to the fridge. If you find peeling and chopping garlic is a hassle each time you want to cook, try this time saving method.

Sauces

These are the common sauces used in Chinese cooking:

Light Soy Sauce

A good quality light soy sauce is important as it can affect the taste of your dish. There are many types of soy sauce in the market. Which soy sauce to use depends on your taste and the ingredients. If you are shopping for light soy sauce, read the label and look for naturally brewed. Avoid any soy sauce with preservatives and coloring. Also you should only use soy sauce made from non-GMO soy beans.

Dark Soy Sauce

Dark soy sauce, also known as old soy sauce, is the darker and thicker version of the light soy sauce. It is richer, tastier and slightly sweeter. Dark soy sauce is mainly used for adding color and flavor to a dish. It is mainly used during the cooking process, rather than after, as its flavor develops during heating.

Oyster Sauce

Oyster sauce is commonly used in Chinese cooking to add a savory flavor to many dishes. It is ideal for flavoring meat and vegetable dishes, also great for noodle stir fries, such as chow mien Traditionally, oyster sauce is made by slowly simmering oysters in water until the juices thicken and caramelized. However, today's oyster sauce used oyster essence or extract, thicken with cornstarch, and darken with caramel. Go for high quality oyster sauce that is naturally dark. I prefer to use non-MSG oyster sauce or vegetarian oyster sauce (made of mushroom extract).

Fermented Bean Paste

Fermented bean paste is made from ground soybeans, which is commonly used in Chinese cuisine in Southeast Asia. The paste is very salty and savory, some varieties spicy. This paste is usually used as condiments to flavor foods such as stir fries and stews.

Basic Cooking Techniques

Stir Frying

This is the most common Chinese cooking method. Woks are ideal for this method of cooking. Stir frying is very quick; therefore, you need to get all the ingredients ready before you start the cooking process.

If you are using any kind of meat, cut them in thin strips so that they can be cooked faster. To make the meat tastier, marinate it with soy sauce and pepper for at least 10 minutes. Long and thin vegetables such as scallions, carrots or asparagus are often cu diagonally so that more surface area is exposed for quicker cooking. As for leafy vegetables, just cut them into bite size pieces. If you are cooking several types of vegetables, you should separate them in different containers. Usually vegetables that cooked slower will be added first. If you are using vegetables that take quite some time to cook, it is better to blanch them in boiling water before cooking.

Once you have everything prepared, heat your wok until it is very hot; then, add a few tablespoonful of oil. Make sure the oil is hot enough before adding your ingredients; otherwise, the food will be greasy. If you are not sure when the oil is hot enough, do dip your spatula or chop sticks into the oil. If you see hot oil bubbles, then the oil is ready. Do not wait too long as the oil can be overheated.

Depending on your taste, the first ingredient to be added is the condiments, such as garlic, onions or ginger to flavor the oil, give them a quick stir. When it becomes aromatic, it is time to add your main ingredients. If you are using meat, always add the meat first as it takes longer time to cook. Then add the vegetables. Stir a while, before adding the seasonings. Add cornstarch if you prefer. There you go, your stir fry dish is ready! Master these basic principles, and you can stir fry any dish you like.

Steaming

This is another favorite cooking technique of mine. I love steaming as the juice and nutrient of the food is contained. This is one of the healthiest method to cook your food. To steam, you can use a bamboo steamer (such as below) or simply use any heat proof plate.

First, boil some water in the wok. Place a steaming rack or any rack stand in the wok. Make sure the water level is below the rack. If your bamboo steamer is big enough, it can stand on its own in the wok without the rack. Make sure the water does not dry up. Do add water for steaming if necessary.

Double steaming or Double boiling

This cooking technique is usually used for preparing delicate food such as bird nest or shark fin soup. Double steaming ensures no loss of liquid or essences of the food being cooked, hence is best for boiling herbal soup. You can easily double steam your soup in a wok, but make sure you cover your soup. Alternatively, use a slow cooker to boil herbal soup. Slow cooker is convenient and you can simply leave the soup to boil for as long as 6 hours on a low flame.

Clay Pot Cooking

Clay pot cooking method used to be very common in Chinese cuisine. However, it was replaced by metal pot when metal pots allow the food to cook quicker. However, many household still prefer cooking in clay pots due to its distinct flavor and nutritional value of the food cooked in them. Pure clay pots cooks the food with far-infrared (FIR) with heat emitted from the walls of the pot. I love clay pots and have various sizes of them. I strongly recommend using clay pot to cook stew or soups.

Feel free to increase or decrease the amount of main ingredients if you want cook more or less. Remember, Chinese cooking is very flexible and feel free to experiment!

Now, let's get on with the recipes.

Terms & Abbreviations

tbs – tablespoon

tsp – teaspoon

cornstarch – 1 tsp of cornflour mixed with 2 tbs of water, stir well. Usually used for thickening sauces or gravy.

Serving size for recipes is 4 unless stated otherwise.

Buttered Prawns With Egg Floss

This is a very popular and common dish in most Chinese restaurants. The aroma of the curry leaves and butter is really amazing. My grandchildren often fight for the egg floss which tastes really delicious and crispy.

Ingredients:

500g prawns

5 egg yolks, beaten

Enough butter to use in frying

20 curry leaves

Evaporated milk

If you like spiciness, do add some small green chilies

Method:

First make the egg floss. Add 3 tbs butter and 2 tbs cooking oil in the wok. Use medium heat to melt the butter. When the oil is hot, pour the yoke in the wok with swirling movement and briskly stirring until it forms into floss and lightly brown. Dish out and spread on a grease proof paper on a plate.

Using the same wok, add another tbs butter and a little cooking oil to mix. Add prawns and fry until cook and crisp. Dish out.

Then scoop another 1 tbs of butter to wok and stir briskly. Fry curry leaves and chopped green chillies if available. Fry till fragrant. Add in evaporated milk, about a quarter can. Add salt and sugar to taste. Keep stirring to mix and bubbling hot. Add in the fried prawns and stir to mix evenly. Dish out on a serving plate. Spread the egg floss on prawns and serve.

Drunken Prawns

Ingredients:

10 tiger prawns, cleaned and veins removed

2 tsp wolf berries (optional)

80 ml Chinese rice wine

Salt and pepper to taste

3 tbs cooking oil

Chopped scallion and parsley

Method:

Marinate the prawns with salt and pepper and rice wine for 10 minutes.

Heat a wok until very hot. Add the oil and swirl to coat. Put in the marinated prawns to fry and turn both sides to cook well. Turn down heat and add in the remainder marinated sauce and simmer slowly until almost dry. Dish out to serve while is still hot. Garnish with chopped scallions and parsley.

Fried Prawns In Tamarind Juice

Ingredients:

300g medium-size prawns, shelled

3 tbs tamarind mixed with 2 tbs hot water

3 tbs oil for frying

cucumber slices to garnish

Method:

Clean prawns by opening a slit at the back to take the veins out. Cut the feelers short. Add about 2 tbs hot water to to mash the tamarind. Put the prawns in to mix evenly and marinate for 1 hour.

Next, heat a non stick pan. Pour enough oil to cover the surface of pan. When the oil is hot, fry the prawns at medium heat until done. Scoop up the prawns and place on a serving plate lined with cucumber.

Stir Fried Clams with Green Mango

I use Asian clams for this dish. This type of clam is easily available in the market. It is important to make sure the clams are fresh. Before cooking, soak the clams in water for 10 minutes to make sure they are free of sand. The picture below shows the clams I used for this dish. You can cook this dish with other types of clam you can get near you.

Ingredients:

500g big clams. rinsed and cleaned

3 small raw mangoes, cut into strips

2 tbs fermented bean paste

2 fresh chillies

3 small onions

1 bulb garlic

3 dry chillies, cut into 1-inch strips

1 big onion, cut to wedges

a few ginger strips

2 tbs cooking oil

3/4 hot cup water

3 stalks of chives, cut into 1 inch-piece

salt and pepper to taste and cornstarch for thickening

Method:

Mince bean paste, small onions, chillies and garlic in a food processor.

Heat oil in a wok and fry the minced ingredients, together with ginger strips and dried chillies until fragrant. Add water and mango strips, stirring to mix. Simmer for a minute. Add the clams and mix evenly with the gravy. Cover and cook for 5 minutes.

Open the cover and stir to make sure the clams are all fully open. Stir in a little cornstarch to thicken gravy.

Add salt and pepper to taste and sprinkle chives, briefly mix and serve.

Prawns in Butter and Cheese Sauce

Ingredients:

10 pieces of big prawns, discard veins, cut off feelers, shelled, leave only the tail

40g butter

100g grated Parmesan cheese or Cheddar cheese

Cornflour with a little water

Half cup evaporated milk

salt and pepper to taste

Method:

Melt butter in a saucepan over gentle heat. Fry the prawns quickly till cooked and fragrant. Dish out and put on a dish. with the same amount of butter add cornflour mixed with a little water to dilute, add half cup evaporated milk and cook gently over fire until thicken. Stir in the cheese until it melts. Add salt and pepper to taste. Pour sauce over prawns and garnish with chopped parsley.

Steamed Squid with Spicy Bean Sauce

Ingredients:

2 large squids, cleaned

1 tbs onion oil (oil fried in slices of small onion)

3 tbs spicy bean paste

1/4 tsp dark soy sauce

1/2 tsp sugar

cornflour with a little water to thicken

chopped coriander

Method:

Put the 2 squids on a plate and steam for 5 minutes. Drain the juice into a bowl. Cut the squids with a scissor into rings and the tentacles shorter. In a sauce pan, add onion oil and add bean paste plus sugar. Pour the juice into the sauce pan. Thicken with a little cornflour mixed with a little water and stir to mix. Pour the sauce over the squid. Garnish with chopped coriander and serve at once.

Grilled Squid

Ingredients:

300g squids, discard heads

Salt and black pepper to taste

Oil for greasing

Lettuce to line the plate

1 lemon, cut into slices to line the plate

Chilli Sauce for dipping:

4 fresh chillies

5 tbs minced garlic and young ginger

Lime juice to taste

Sugar to taste

Method:

First, prepare the chilli sauce. Mince ingredients for chilli sauce and add lime juice and sugar to taste. Put aside.

Slit open and flatten the squid on the cutting board, lightly cut the surface diagonally. Heat griddle or pan until very hot. Add oil to grease. Put the squids on top and cook both sides till done. It will curl a little and turn a little brown when cooked. Lay the cleaned lettuce on a plate, place the grilled squids on top. Garnish with lemon slices. Dip in chili sauce or serve with rice.

Spicy Fish Stew With Bean Sauce

For this recipe, you can fish such as sea bass, halibut, or red snapper.

Ingredients:

1 fish (cleaned and cut into big slices)

4 or 5 dried chillies, cut into 1-inch piece

2 big onions, cut into wedges

5 slices of ginger

1 cup oil for frying

1 tbs oyster sauce

1 tbs fermented bean paste

1 table light soy sauce

1 tsp dark soy sauce

1 cup water

1 tbs cornflour to mix in a little water

2 stalks of scallions, 2 inches

Method:

Add oil in a wok. When oil is hot, fry fish pieces evenly till light brown. Dish out and put aside.

Discard oil and remain just 2 tbs oil in the wok. Fry onions, ginger and chillies till fragrant. Add in the bean paste, stir fry to mix and add 1 cup water. Put in the fish and a mixture of light and dark soy sauce and oyster sauce.

Simmer in low flame for half an hour or till the meat is soft and smooth to taste. Stir in cornstarch to thicken the gravy. Sprinkle in the scallions. Add salt and pepper to taste. Stir to mix and dish out on a plate to serve.

Steamed Fried Fish Rolls with Asparagus

Ingredients:

300g asparagus cut into 2 inch length

1 packet fish paste

5 Chinese mushrooms, soaked until soft, rinsed

2 fresh chillies sliced thinly

Some sliced scallion

1 tbs chopped garlic and ginger

2 tbs oil

1 tbs soy sauce

Salt and pepper to taste

Cornstarch

Method:

Blanche asparagus in hot water and put aside. Cut mushroom into thin strips.

On a clean cutting board, spread fish paste about 2 inch wide and about 3 inch length. Put a strip of mushroom, a slice of chili and scallion. Then roll the fish paste. Continue to do until all the fish paste has finished. Put them neatly on a plate greased with a little oil. Steam for 10 minutes in a steamer.

In a wok, fry the chopped garlic and ginger until fragrant. Stir in the asparagus and fish rolls. Add a little water and cornflour to make a thick gravy. Add soy sauce, salt and pepper to taste. Simmer for a minute. Dish out to serve.

Steamed Prawns With Ginger

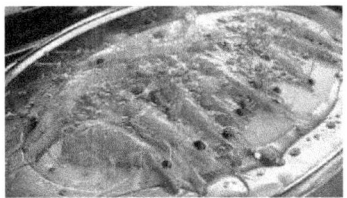

Ingredients:

10 big tiger prawns, removed veins, cut off feelers, shelled

2 tbs minced young fresh ginger

2 tbs ginger wine

salt and pepper to taste

a few dash of sesame oil

chopped parsley

Method:

Put the cleaned prawns on a heat proof plate. Add chopped ginger, wine, salt and pepper to taste. Put in a wok of boiling water and cover to steam for 10 minutes. Add some chopped parsley and sesame oil. Serve with rice.

Stir Fried Prawns with Sweet Plum Sauce

Ingredients:

300g fresh water prawns, removed veins

2 tbs cooking oil

1 tbs chopped garlic and ginger

2 stalk of scallions (cut into 2 inches length)

1/2 cup of plum sauce

2 tbs water

sugar and salt to taste

Method:

Add oil in a wok and when hot add prawns and fry for 3 min. Move the prawns to the side of wok and fry ginger and garlic till fragrant. Add the scallion and toss to mix well for 2 min.

Add plum sauce mix with water, sugar and salt to taste. Stir well until prawns are well coated, for about 5 minutes. Serve with rice.

Pan Fried Red Snapper with Tamarind Sauce

Ingredient:

2 slices of red snapper

4 tbs oil for frying

Salt and pepper to taste

1 big onion , sliced

2 red chillies, sliced

1 tsp dried shrimp powder

2 tbs tamarind paste, mix with little water to obtain the juice

1 tsp light soy sauce

1 tsp sugar

Method:

In a frying pan, heat the oil till hot and fry the fish on both the sides. Transfer fish on to a serving dish. Pour out the oil and leave 1 tsp oil on frying pan. Add in the big onion slices and fry till soft. Mix in the dry shrimp powder, soy sauce, tamarind juice and sugar. Simmer for a while and add chilly slices. Pour the sauce over fish and serve.

Crispy Coconut Prawns

Ingredients:

300g grated coconut

20 big prawns

1 stalk lemongrass, finely grounded

1/2 tsp coriander leaves

1/2 turmeric powder

1/2 tsp sugar

1/2 tsp salt

Method:

Season prawns with lemongrass, coriander, turmeric powder, sugar and salt. Leave aside for half an hour. Coat with the grated coconut and deep-fried in hot oil till crispy. Dish out, drain the oil and serve.

Steamed Cod Fish With Mushroom

If you are looking for healthy ways to cook cod, try steaming. Steaming retains the juice and freshness of the fish. Please note that steamed fish must be served immediately. The fish will taste fishy if the dish gets cold.

Ingredients:

300g cod fillet

2 big dried mushrooms, soaked and cut into strips

1 tbs ginger strips

1 tbs light soy sauce

1 tbs fish sauce

1/4 cup water

2 tbs rice wine

1 tbs sesame oil

Red chilies strips for garnishing

Method:

Rinse cod and put on a heat proof plate. Add water into the wok and bring to boil on high heat. Put cod on a steamer and cover lid. Steam for 12 minutes on high heat.

Meanwhile, in a sauce pan, add sesame oil and ginger strips, mushrooms and stir fry for 30 seconds. Then, add water, soy sauce and fish sauce. Bring to a boil and simmer to low heat. Add rice wine, salt, pepper and strips of chili. Stir to mix and pour over the cod. Garnish with parsley if you wish. Serve immediately.

Nourishing Herbal Steamed Fish

The Chinese herbs used are commonly found in any Chinese medical halls or shops. For convenience, buy the prepacked ones.

Ingredients:

500g White Pomfret (or other fish of your choice),cleaned

10g yuk chuk (Solomon's Seal Rhizome), cut into 2 inch length

10g dang shen (or Codonopsis pilosula), cut into 1 inch length

10g pak kei (or Astragalus Root)

1 table spoon wolf berries

3 red dates, cut into halves

500g chicken broth

2 tbs minced ginger

1 tbs light soy sauce

1 tbs sesame oil

2 tbs cooking oil

Salt and pepper to taste

Scallions and parsley to garnish

Method:

Blanche the fish with boiling water and set aside. Add oil, minced ginger, light soy sauce to fish. Put in the fish to steam at moderate heat.

Meanwhile boil the herbs in chicken broth for 20 minutes. Put in 2 tbs rice wine. Add salt and a dash of pepper to taste. Pour broth on to the fish and continue to steam for further 15 minutes on medium heat. Garnish and serve.

Prawns and Vegetables Salad

Ingredients:

300g prawn, peeled and removed veins

1 cucumber, cut In cubes

1 red bell pepper, cut in cubes

1 tbs sweet relish, (available in supermarkets)

1 tbs lime juice

2 tbs mayonnaise

Pepper and salt to taste

1 tsp olive oil

2 cups cooked rice

2 tbs chopped chives for garnishing

Method:

Blanch prawns in boiling water until cooked. Remove and drain. In a mixing bowl, place prawns and vegetables and mix well with mayonnaise and lime juice and oil. Add pepper and salt to taste.

Stir Fried Cuttlefish

This cuttlefish used in this recipe is the dried type which need to be soaked to soften. It is sold in most wet markets or hypermarkets.

Ingredients:

500 cuttlefish

3 thin slices ginger

1 tbs minced garlic

2 stalks scallions, cut into 2 cm length

salt and pepper to taste

2 tbs rice wine

Dash of vinegar

Method:

In a sauce pan, bring water to boil. Blanch squids or cuttlefish in hot water. Both will immediately roll and curl up and put aside. Heat a wok, fry garlic, ginger and scallion for one minute and add in the cuttlefish. stir fry and add wine, salt and pepper to taste. Add a dash of vinegar and heat through. Remove and serve.

King Prawns in Hoisin Sauce With Sesame Seed

Ingredients:

12 large prawns, remove veins, shelled

1 tsp sesame oil

4 tbs cornflour

4 tbs cooking oil

1 large onion thinly sliced

2 tbs Hoisin sauce

½ tsp sugar

2 tbs sesame seeds, toasted

Salt and pepper to taste

1 tbs chopped scallion and parsley

Method:

Marinate prawns with salt, pepper, and also sesame oil for 30 minutes. Dust prawns with cornflour. Add 4 tbs oil in a heated pan and fry the prawns for 3 minutes on each side. Remove and put aside.

Reduce oil to 1 tbs. Fry onions slices till fragrant, add in Hoisin sauce and sugar. Simmer sauce until thicken. Add salt and pepper to taste. Pour sauce over prawns and garnish with sesame seeds, scallion and parsley.

Deep Fried Black Pomfret in Tangy Sauce

Ingredients:

600g Black Pomfret

Oil for deep-frying

1 tbs salt

2 tbs cornstarch

1 tbs garlic

1 red chilly, seeded and sliced

Chopped scallion and parsley for garnishing

Sauce:

3 tbs fish sauce

3 tbs freshly squeezed lemon juice or orange juice

3 tbs sugar

1 tsp sesame oil

Method:

Make a diagonal cut on both sides of fish. Rub salt evenly on both sides of it and dab cornflour all over fish. Heat enough oil until very hot. Deep fry fish until olden brown. Remove and place fish on a serving dish. Remove excess oil and leave one tablespoon. Fry garlic until fragrant and add chilli and the prepared sauce. Simmer for 2 minutes and pour the sauce over fish. Garnish with chopped scallions and parsley before serving.

Deep Fried Honey Sesame Prawns

Ingredients:

1 kg big prawns, peeled, removed veins with tails intact

250g honey

2 tbs toasted sesame seeds

Oil for deep frying

2 tsp lemon juice

1 tsp sweet chili sauce

2 scallion thinly sliced

2 beaten eggs

2 tbs cornflour

Method:

Heat a wok and pour in enough oil and wait till is very hot. Meanwhile, place the beaten eggs, cornflour and half tsp salt in a bowl and whisk till smooth.

Dip the prawns into the batter up to the tail and carefully lower into the wok. Cook in patches for about 5 minutes or until cooked and brown. Place the prawns on the serving dish.

In a sauce pan, put honey, chili sauce, lemon juice and 1 tbs water and mix well. Simmer over medium heat until the sauce thickens slightly and spread sauce over prawns. Sprinkle with sesame seeds and top with scallions.

Stir Fried Abalone With Broccoli

Ingredients:

1 tin of abalone

200g broccoli, soaked, drain and floret

2 tbs cooking oil

1 tsp cornflour mixed with a little water

1 tbs oyster sauce

1 tsp soy sauce

1 tsp chopped garlic and ginger

100 ml water

Method:

Cut the abalone into thin slices and keep the stock in a bowl. Heat a wok and add in oil and swirl round to coat.

Fry the ginger and garlic for a while and add in slices of abalone, soy sauce, oyster sauce, and stock and water. Simmer for 5 to 10 minutes.

Thicken the gravy with cornflour mixture. Simmer to heat through. In another pot blanch broccoli in hot water for 3 seconds and line dish with broccoli. Scoop abalone on the plate and serve while is hot.

Savoury Sardines In Tomato Sauce

Ingredients:

1 large tin sardines

2 large sliced onions

3 sliced red chillies

1 tbs thick soy sauce mixed with 1/2 cup water

1 tsp lime juice

2 to 4 tbs tomato sauce or to taste

Method:

Heat oil in a pan and fry the onions and red chillies. Add sardines and keep stirring for a minute. Add the soy sauce and tomato sauce. Simmer for about 10 minutes. Add lime juice and mixed. Dish out to serve with bread or rice.

Braised Crab in Clay Pot

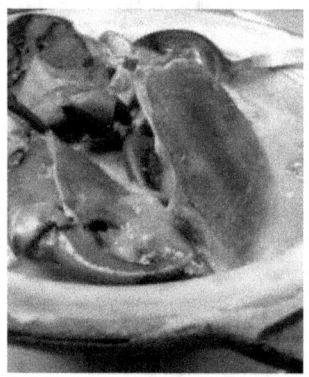

Ingredients:

1 kg crabs, scrub the shells and claws cleaned, and crack

1 tbs finely chopped garlic

3 tbs oil

1 tsp pepper corn, crushed

8 small chillies

3 to 4 pieces fragrant lime leaves

1 cube chicken stock- boil with 4 cups water

4 Chinese celery roots, lightly crushed

1 can evaporated milk

1 tsp fish sauce

Chinese celery and scallions to garnish – finely cut

Method:

Heat 3 tbs oil in a sauce pan and fry the garlic till fragrant. Put a side. Stir in pepper corn, celery root, lime leaves and fry awhile. Transfer into a large shallow clay pot, add in chicken stock and crabs. Cover clay pot and boil on high heat for 5 minutes. Add evaporated milk and fish sauce and salt to taste. Bring to the boil and garnish with celery and scallion before serving.

Fried Crab In Black Pepper Sauce

This is a delicious way to cook the crabs. The strong flavor and aroma of the black pepper enhance the taste of the crab.

Ingredients:

500g crabs, cleaned, cut into pieces

Oil for deep frying

Some corn flour to dust the crabs

4 tbs black pepper sauce

1 tbs freshly minced garlic

2 tbs shredded scallion and red chillies

1 tbs corn flour mix with 2 tbs water

1/2 tbs sugar

1/2 cup water

Method:

Dust crabs with cornflour. Heat a wok until very hot. Pour enough oil to deep fry crabs until golden yellow. Drain.

Pour out excess oil and leave 2 tbs in the wok. Fry minced garlic for 1 second and add black pepper sauce. stir fry awhile. Add water and bring to boil. Stir in cornflour mixture and sugar.

Heat through and garnish with scallion and chillies.

Deep Fried Stuffed Squid

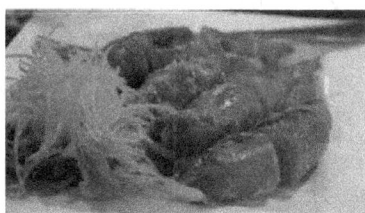

Ingredients:

500g squid, cleaned with tentacles attached

100g fish paste

salt and pepper to taste

1 beaten egg

enough cornflour to coat

enough oil for frying

Method:

Combine fish paste, salt and pepper in a mixing bowl. Stuff fish paste into squids, leaving only 3/4 full. Secure tentacles with toothpicks.

Dip the squids into the beaten eggs and then coat squids in cornflour. Heat a wok until very hot and put in enough oil to fry squids until they are cooked and light brown in color. Place squids on the plate, garnished with cucumber slices and serve.

Steamed Halibut With Szechuan Cabbage

Ingredients:

2 slices halibut

3 thin slices fresh ginger, cut into thin strips

1 soaked Chinese mushroom, cleaned and cut to thin strips

2 tbs shredded Szechuan cabbage

1 scallion, about 1-inch length

1 tbs cooked lean pork, shredded

Salt, pepper and sugar to taste

1 tbs light soy sauce

1 tsp cornflour with 1 tbs water to mix

Coriander leaves to garnish

Method:

Place the halibut ready on the plate. Add the shredded cabbage, pork, ginger strips and the rest of the ingredients in a bowl. Mix well together and heap on to the halibut slices. Steam for about 15 minutes. Garnish with coriander leaves and serve hot.

Fish Fillet with Tangy Orange Sauce

Ingredients :

1 piece fish fillet (about 250g)

1 cup of oil deep-frying

2 slices ginger

200ml fresh orange juice

1 tbs lemon juice

1 tbs shredded lemon rind

Seasoning :

2 tbs sugar

1/2 tbs salt

Method :

Marinate the fish fillet with a little salt and pepper for 10 minutes. Coat lightly with cornflour and deep fry in hot oil until golden brown. Dish out and drain the oil.

Leave 1 tbs of oil in the wok and fry the ginger until fragrant. Add in orange juice, lemon juice, 1 teaspoon sugar and bring to boil again. Make sure you lower the heat, then add in fried fish and shredded lemon rind and simmer for 15 minutes or until the gravy is thick.

Place the fried fillet on a plate, and pour the sauce over it. Garnish with some sliced red chilli and parsley.

Thai Style Steamed Fish

Ingredients:

1 fleshy fish (about 600g) and cleaned

1 tbs of oil

1 tbs chopped fragrant galangal

2 stalks lemongrass – crushed it

1/2 tbs chopped spicy hot small chili

5 preserved plums

1 tomato cut into wedges

50g preserved green mustard – shredded and soaked

150ml water

Seasoning :

1 tbs Thai chili paste

1 tbs sugar

1/2 tbs light soy sauce

1 tbs rice wine

A dash of sesame oil and pepper.

Method :

Heat oil and stir fry chopped galangal, lemongrass and chopped chili. Stir fry until fragrant. Add in the remaining ingredients and seasoning. Then let it simmer for 5 minutes.

Place the fish in the steamer and steam at high heat for 15 minutes. Then pour away the water. Pour the sauce over the fish and sprinkle chopped parsley on top and serve.

Note: Galangal, also known as blue ginger, is related to the ginger family. It has a similar flavor but much more potent. The fresh galangal is very hard and slicing it requires a sharp knife. Here's a picture of galangal.

Prawn Bean Curd Stew In Clay Pot

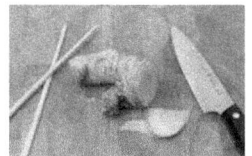

Ingredients:

2 fried bean curd, cut into 4 parts each

200g medium prawns

1 tbs bean paste

1 tbs chopped garlic

1 sprig scallion cut into 1 inch length

1 chili, cut into strips

1/2 tsp sugar

50g snow peas

30g carrots cut into strips

1 tsp cornflour mixed water to thicken gravy

1/4 cup water

Method:

Add 2 tbs oil in a wok. When hot , fry the chopped garlic and bean paste till fragrant. Add prawns and fry a few minutes and put in a clay pot Add half cup water. Cover and cook for about 5 minutes. Lift up cover and add sugar and salt to taste. Thicken gravy with cornflour mixture. Put in snow peas, carrot strips, scallion and chili strips. Serve the bean curd bubbling hot in the clay pot

Tamarind Stingray Curry

Ingredients: 6 servings

600 gm stingray fish, rinsed

2 tomatoes, cut into wedges

300 gm lady's fingers

4 lemon grass, cut finely

1 big piece fresh turmeric, 3 inches

15 small onions

1 clove garlic, smashed

10 fresh chillies

Chilli paste, add to taste

1 piece toasted shrimp paste, 3cm square

4 tbs oil

4 fragrant lime leaves

Sweet basil ,

2 red ginger flower bud (torch ginger), cut finely

Tamarind juice, add to taste

2 liters water

Sugar and salt, add to taste

Method:

Blanch ladies fingers in hot water and put aside.

Blend onions, garlic, chillies, lemon grass, turmeric and shrimp paste. In a wok, add oil and fry the blended ingredients until fragrant. Add the sweet basil and fragrant lime leaves and ginger plant bud.

Add tamarind paste mix with water as desired. Bring to boil. Add in fish and simmer in low heat until the fish is cooked. Add sugar and salt to taste. Serve with rice.

Fried Red Snapper In Sauce

Ingredients:

2 slices red snapper

4 tbs oil for frying

salt and pepper to taste

1 big onion, sliced

2 red chillies, sliced

1 tsp shrimp paste powder

1 tbs tamarind juice (tamarind paste mix with little water to obtain the juice)

1 tsp light soy sauce

1 tbs tomato sauce

1 tsp sugar

Method:

In a frying pan, heat the oil till very hot and deep fry the fish till golden brown. Dish out and transfer fish on to a serving dish.

Reduce the oil to 1 tsp oil on frying pan. Add in the onion and fry till soft. Mix in shrimp paste powder, soya sauce, tamarind juice, tomato sauce and sugar. Simmer for a while and add chilli slices. Pour sauce over fish and serve.

Super Stuffed Crab Meat Mushrooms

1-1/2 pound large mushrooms

1 can crab meat or 6 oz fresh crab meat

1/4 cup paleo mayonnaise

1 teaspoon lemon juice

1 teaspoon grated onion

2 tablespoons minced mushroom stems

1/2 teaspoon salt

1/2 teaspoon black pepper

1/2 pound bacon

Preheat oven to 350 degrees.

Clean mushrooms, remove stems, minced, and reserve.

In a large bowl, mix crabmeat, mayonnaise, lemon juice, onion, minced mushroom stems, salt and black pepper.

Fill cavities of mushrooms with mixture. Wrap with half a slice of bacon and fasten with a toothpick.

Place on cookie sheet and bake for 15 to 20 minutes or until bacon is crisp.

Remove and place on absorbent paper.

Serve warm.

Fast And Furious Shrimp

1 lb Wild Caught Shrimp

1 bag frozen roasted red bell peppers & onions

or 1 bell pepper diced and 1/2 yellow onion diced

4 big hand fulls of baby spinach leaves

2 tablespoons coconut oil

2 tablespoons coconut milk

1/4 tablespoon curry powder

Sea salt and black pepper to taste

In a large skillet, heat the coconut oil over medium heat. Add the onions and bell peppers and cook until defrosted and sizzling if using the frozen or until the veggies become tender if using fresh. Add the shrimp and the spinach and cook for 3-4 minutes or until the shrimp curls up and is no longer opaque in the middle. Add the coconut milk and spices, mix well and serve!

Island Soul Seafood Stew

3 lbs of raw seafood

1 yellow onion, diced

5 cloves garlic, minced

2 tablespoons cumin

1 bunch cilantro

3 tomatoes, chopped

1 can coconut milk

1 tbsp coconut oil

Add: Sea salt and black pepper to taste.

Dice up the stems of the cilantro bunch then set aside.

In a large soup pot saute the onions in the coconut oil.

When the onions start to turn brown, add the garlic and the cilantro stems and saute for another 2-3 onions.

Add the tomatoes, cumin, salt and pepper, mix well and cook for another 2-3 minutes. Add the coconut milk and bring to a simmer.

Add the seafood then cook for another 3-6 minutes or until the seafood is done.

Hawaiian Mushrooms Stuffed with Crab

8 ounces canned crab meat

3 dozen large fresh mushrooms

1 tablespoon parsley, finely minced

1 tablespoon chopped pimiento (pepper)

1/4 teaspoon dry mustard

1/4 cup paleo mayonnaise

Remove stems from mushrooms.

Combine crab, parsley, and pimiento.

Blend mustard into mayonnaise. Toss into crab mixture.

Fill each mushroom crown with about 2 tablespoons crab mixture.

Bake at 375°F (190°C) for 8 to 10 minutes.

Belgian Endive Stuffed with Crabmeat Ravigote

1/2 cup mayonnaise

2 teaspoons Dijon mustard

2 teaspoons fresh lemon juice

1/2 teaspoon minced garlic

1/4 teaspoon hot red pepper sauce

3/4 teaspoon salt

2 tablespoons chopped green onions

1/4 cup seeded, small diced tomatoes

2 tablespoons small capers, drained

1 tablespoon minced shallots

1 tablespoon chopped fresh parsley

1 pound lump crabmeat, picked over for shells and cartilage

4 heads Belgian endive, cored, leaves separated and wiped clean

1 head radicchio Treviso, cored, leaves separated and wiped clean

2 bunches fresh watercress, garnish

In a bowl, combine the mayonnaise, mustard, lemon juice, garlic, hot sauce, and salt. Whisk to combine. Fold in the green onions, tomatoes, capers, shallots, and parsley. Gently fold in the crabmeat, turning to gently coat with the dressing and being careful not to break up the lumps. Adjust seasoning, to taste.

Spoon a heaping tablespoon of the stuffing into endive and radicchio leaves. Arrange the watercress and stuffed endives and radicchio decoratively on a platter and serve as an hors d'oeuvre. Alternately, place the watercress on 10 small plates and drizzle with extra-virgin olive oil

Steam Red Pepper Shellfish (Mussels)

5 pounds mussels

3 sprigs fresh tarragon

5 sprigs fresh flat-leaf parsley, plus more chopped for garnish

1 750-ml bottle dry white wine

2 1/2 cups water

3 tablespoons freshly squeezed lemon juice

2 shallots, sliced

18 whole black peppercorns

2 tablespoons coarse salt

1 large red bell pepper

Rémoulade Sauce

Discard any mussels with broken shells. To clean mussels, soak them in cold water for 15 minutes, and scrub shells with a stiff brush. Using your thumb and forefinger, grasp the dark, weedy growth (the beard) protruding from between the mussel shells, and tug it from the mussel. Rinse well, and refrigerate until needed.

Make a bouquet garni: Tie tarragon and parsley sprigs in a small piece of cheesecloth, and set aside. Combine wine, water, lemon juice, shallots, peppercorns, salt, and bouquet garni in a large stockpot with a tight-fitting lid. Bring to a boil, then simmer over low heat for 15 minutes.

Add mussels, and cover. Increase heat to medium, and cook, shaking occasionally, until the mussels open, 5 to 7 minutes.

Remove mussels from broth, and cool both separately. Discard any shells that haven't opened, as well as the half shell to which mussel isn't attached. When cool, put mussels back into broth, cover, and chill until ready to serve. This can be done 1 to 2 days before serving.

Place red pepper directly over the trivet of a gas-stove burner on high heat or on a grill. Just as each section turns puffy and black, turn the pepper with tongs to prevent overcooking. (If you don't have a gas stove, place the pepper on a baking pan, and broil in the oven, turning as each side becomes charred.) Place pepper in a paper bag to cool. Peel and seed pepper; cut in 1/2-inch-wide strips, then into diamonds.

Cut mussels from shells with a paring knife. Pour a little remoulade sauce in each shell, and garnish with chopped parsley and a red-pepper diamond.

Pass on a tray with toothpicks or wooden forks.

Mussels Vinaigrette

24 medium mussels

1/2 cup olive oil

3 tablespoons red wine vinegar or lemon juice

1 teaspoon capers, chopped if large

1 tablespoon minced onion

1 tablespoon minced pimiento

1 tablespoon minced parsley

salt

fresh ground pepper

1 slice lemon

Scrub mussels well and remove the beards.

Discard any that do not close tightly, set aside.

Whisk the oil and vinegar together in a bowl, then add capers, onion, pimiento, parsley, salt and pepper to taste.

Place one cup water in a frypan with the lemon slice.

Add the mussels and bring to a boil.

Remove the mussels as they open; cool.

Remove the mussel meat from the shells, reserving half the shells, and mix it into the vinaigrette.

Cover and refrigerate overnight.

Clean the reserved mussel shells well and place them in a plastic bag in the refrigerator.

Before serving, replace the mussels in the shells and spoon a small amount of the vinaigrette over.

Thai-Style Mussels with Pickled Ginger

2 teaspoons oil

1/2 cup minced shallots

1 tablespoon chile paste with garlic

1 garlic clove, minced

1/2 cup light coconut milk

1/4 teaspoon lime rind

1/4 cup fresh lime juice

1/4 cup minced pickled ginger

1/4 cup chopped fresh parsley

2 pounds mussels, scrubbed and debearded (about 40 mussels)

Parsley sprigs (optional)

Heat the oil in a large Dutch oven over medium-high heat. Add the shallots, chile paste, and garlic; cook 2 minutes or until tender, stirring constantly. Add coconut milk and next 5 ingredients (coconut milk through mussels); bring to a boil. Cover and cook 5 minutes or until shells open.

Remove from heat; discard any unopened shells. Garnish with parsley sprigs, if desired.

Broiled Mussels with Sweet Paprika Aioli

1 1/2 pounds mussels

Sweet Paprika Aioli

1 tablespoon fresh Italian parsley, coarsely chopped

1 1/2 teaspoons freshly squeezed lemon juice

Heat the oven to 400°F and arrange a rack in the middle. Scrub the mussels and debeard them by grabbing the thread, or beard, that runs along the side of the shell and removing it by pulling it toward the hinge of the shell.

Spread the mussels on a baking sheet in a single layer and roast until they open, about 3 to 5 minutes. Remove from the oven and let cool for about 5 minutes. Discard any unopened mussels. Heat the broiler to high.

Carefully pull apart the mussel shells and discard the meatless side of each. With your fingers or a teaspoon, carefully detach the meat from each shell, place it back in the shell, and return the mussel to the baking sheet. Top each mussel with 1/2 teaspoon aioli.

Broil the mussels until the aioli is browned, about 2 to 3 minutes. Remove from the oven, sprinkle with parsley, and drizzle with lemon juice. Serve immediately.

Avocado and Shrimp Rafts

2 large red bell peppers

1 avocado, halved, pitted and peeled

1 tablespoon lime juice

1/4 teaspoon salt

14 medium-sized cooked shrimp (about 12 ounces) split lengthwise

1/3 cup prepared salsa

In a small bowl, combine avocado with lime juice and salt; mash until mixture is chunky. In another small bowl, combine shrimp and salsa. Arrange pepper squares on work surface, skin side down. Spoon avocado mixture on squares, dividing evenly; top each with half a shrimp and a cilantro leaf, if desired. Cover surface with plastic wrap and refrigerate until ready to serve.

Shrimp-Stuffed Avocados

2 ripe, fresh avocados*, seeded

2 Tbsp. fresh lime juice

1 lb. baby shrimp (can substitute crab meat)

1/2 small red onion, finely diced (can be overpowering, try Vidella)

2 mangoes, peeled, seeded and diced

1/2 cup paleo mayonnaise

1/2 tsp. salt

1/4 tsp. freshly ground black pepper

1/4 cup chopped chives

Boston or other lettuce leaves, optional, for serving

Using a large spoon, scoop out the avocado from each half and cut into small dice. Place avocado pieces in a medium mixing bowl and toss with lime juice.

Add shrimp, onion, mango, mayonnaise, salt, pepper and half the chives.

Stir gently to combine well.

Fill avocado halves with even amounts of shrimp mixture. Place each half on plate with lettuce. Sprinkle with remaining chives and serve.

*Large avocados are recommended for this recipe. A large avocado averages about 8 ounces. If using smaller or larger size avocados adjust the quantity accordingly.

Shrimp Stuffed Avocados

3 avocados

1/2 green onion (optional)

2 tsp. paleo mayonnaise

1 lemon (or less)

1/4 lb. cooked shrimp

salt and pepper

Open the Avocados. Cut the avocado lengthwise all the way around. Twist the halves and using your knife, strike and remove the pit. With a spoon remove the avocado from the peel and place it in a large mixing bowl. Do this with all the avocados. Mash the avocado pulp, use a potato masher to slightly mash the avocados so they still have chunks in it. Arrange shells on serving dish.

Cut the green onion into thin strips. Add this to the avocado mixture.

Season the avocado with some salt and pepper. Squeeze half the lemon into the bowl. Next add the mayonnaise and combine this all together. You can add the shrimp whole (don't forget to reserve 6 shrimps for the top of each avocado), or first give them a rough chop. Put the shrimp into the bowl, then mix it all together. Scoop the mixture back into the shells of the avocados, top each with a whole shrimp. Chill an hour and then serve.

Shrimp Stuffed Grape Leaves

20 jarred grape leaves

2 Tablespoons extra virgin olive oil

6 cloves garlic, peeled and chopped

1 1/2 teaspoons chili paste (ideally Sambal Oelek Sauce)

1 pound raw shrimp, peeled and deveined, tail removed

2 Tablespoons pure fish sauce, e.g. Red Boat Fish Sauce

1 cup unsweetened, flaked coconut

6 radishes, minced

8 scallions, chopped

1/4 cup fresh basil, chopped

1 Tablespoon fresh lime juice

Sauce

1 ripe mango

3/4 cup paleo mayonnaise

Remove the grape leaves from the jar, unroll and separate them, and rinse them well under cold water. Leave them to soak while doing the rest of the preparation.

Heat the olive oil in a large skillet and saute the garlic for one minute.

Add the chili paste and saute quickly until it bubbles, about 30 seconds.

Add the shrimp and cook for three minutes, until they begin to turn pink.

Stir in the fish sauce and coconut and continue cooking for 2 minutes longer, until the shrimp are tender. Remove from the heat.

Puree half of the shrimp mixture in a food processor. Coarsely chop the other half of he mixture. Stir both mixtures together with the basil and the lime juice.

Drain the grape leaves and pat dry. Place the first leaf on a flat surface.

On the middle of the leaf place 1/2 teaspoon radish, 1 teaspoon green onion, and 1 rounded teaspoon shrimp mixture. Form this into a packet by folding each side of the leaf over the filling. Roll the blunt end of the leaf toward the pointed end until a packet is formed. Place this into a steamer basket. Repeat the process until all the leaves have been used. Put the basket on to steam over plain water for 10 minutes.

While the packets are steaming, prepare the sauce. Peel the mango and cut away all the fleah. Puree the flesh in a food processor. Remove the puree to a bowl andstir in the mayonnaise until thoroughly blended.

Serve warm, with sauce on the side.

Prawn Cocktail

1 ripe avocado

1 lemon

1/2 lb of cooked small peeled prawns

Lemon wedges, to garnish

1/2 iceberg lettuce

For the Marie Rose Sauce:

7 oz paleo mayonnaise

2-3 tbsp paleo tomato ketchup

Pinch cayenne pepper

Dash Tabasco, to taste

Cut the avocado in half, remove the stone and carefully score each half using a small knife to create a criss-cross pattern. Squeeze each half generously with lemon juice to prevent it from dis-colouring.

To make the Marie Rose sauce mix the mayonnaise, ketchup, cayenne pepper, and a squeeze of lemon juice together in a large bowl. Season to taste with

Tabasco. Stir to combine.

Place a spoonful of Marie Rose sauce into the bottom of 4 serving glasses.

Shred the lettuce and divide equally among the glasses. Scrape out the flesh from the avocado using a spoon and scatter over the lettuce. Spoon another layer of sauce on top.

Arrange the prawns on top and finish with a final spoonful of sauce (reserving any remaining sauce for future use). Sprinkle with a touch of cayenne pepper and garnish with a lemon wedge in each glass to serve.

Lucious Lime Shrimp

3 T fresh lime juice

1 green onion, chopped

2 T chopped fresh cilantro

1 t minced, seeded jalapeno

1 t olive oil

1/2 t minced garlic

20 large shrimp (about a pound) peeled and de-veined

1 T minced red pepper

20 cucumber slices

Stir together lime juice, green onion, cilantro, jalapeno, oil, and garlic in medium bowl. Toss the shrimp with 2 tablespoons of the dressing in another medium bowl. Cover and refrigerate shrimp for 30 minutes. Preheat broiler (or grill). Broil shrimp about 3 inches from heat for 1 1/2 minutes per side or until opaque. Immediately toss hot shrimp with the remaining dressing and red pepper and cool to room temperature. Arrange shrimp on cucumber slices. Make 22 appetizers.

Low-Carb Coconut Shrimp

1 pound large raw shrimp, peeled and deveined (thaw if frozen)

1/3 cup coconut flour

1/4 teaspoon cayenne pepper, or 1 teaspoon ancho pepper

1/4 teaspoon black pepper

1 teaspoon salt

2 eggs

2 tablespoons water

1/2 cup shredded coconut - unsweetened

cooking oil of your choice

Mix coconut flour with red and black peppers, and salt.

Whisk the eggs with a fork in a small dish, and mix with the 2 tb water.

Put shredded coconut in a separate dish.

Put oil in a large skillet to about 3/4 inch depth. Heat to 350 to 360 degrees, or until the end of a wooden spoon handle dipped into the oil collects bubbles around it.

Holding shrimp by the tail, roll in coconut flour, and shake to get most of it off - you just want a thin coating. Then dip in egg, again shaking off the excess. Finally, roll in coconut.

Fry the shrimp until golden on each side, about 2 minutes per side. I usually put each in the pan as I prepare them, but you have to watch the ones in the pan closely if you do it this way. An alternative is to bread a few at once and then put them all in the pan at the same time. Don't crowd the pan, which will lower the temperature of the oil - this makes them absorb more oil and end up heavy and greasy. Tongs are the best tool for turning and removing the shrimp.

Remove from the pan to a paper towel or cooling rack.

Gluten Free Coconut Shrimp

2 pounds large tiger prawns or shrimp, peeled and deviened

2/3 cup coconut flour

1/2 teaspoon cayenne pepper

1 teaspoon garlic powder

2 eggs, beaten

1 1/2 cups shredded coconut

1/4 cup almond flour

salt and pepper to taste

Heat the oven to 425 degrees. Prepare a baking sheet with parchment paper.

Put ingredients into three bowls as follows -- dish #1- coconut flour, cayenne pepper, garlic powder; dish #2- eggs; dish #3-coconut, almond flour, salt and pepper. Dip each shrimp first into dish #1, then #2, then #3.

Place shrimp on the prepared baking sheet.

Coconut Shrimp

1 pound of shrimp, deveined and peeled

2 cups of flaked unsweetened coconut (works better than shredded)

1/4 cup of almond milk

2 egg whites, whisked really well until frothy (helps the coconut stick)

1/3 cup coconut flour

1/4 tsp of cayenne pepper (or more if you want a bite)

1/4 tsp of sea salt

Preheat the oven at 400 degrees

Place parchment paper on a baking sheet (or simply grease one).

Prepare three bowls:

One with frothy egg whites and almond milk

One with coconut flour, salt and cayenne pepper

One with flaked coconut

Dip the cleaned shrimp into the flour, then the egg whites, then finally the shredded coconut. Place coconut covered shrimp on baking sheet. Once the sheet is full, pop the shrimp in the oven until they start to brown (about 15 minutes)

Low Carb Coconut Battered Shrimp

2 eggs

2 1/2 tbsp coconut flour (I didn't sift it)

1/4 tsp of baking powder

dash of Salt and pepper

1 tsp of your preferred seasoning *optional

8 medium sized shrimp, without the shell

1/2 cup or more of unsweetened coconut flakes

Preheat your deep fryer to 325 F.

In a bowl whisk the eggs.

Add the coconut flour, baking powder, salt and pepper, and any additional seasoning.

Mix until the batter is smooth.

Put the shredded coconut flakes in a separate bowl.

This part gets messy. One at a time, place the shrimp in the batter and using your hands mold the batter around the shrimp and then immediately dip the batter covered shrimp in the coconut flakes.

Press the coconut flakes all over the shrimp and set aside.

Repeat for each shrimp.

Place about 3-4 shrimp at a time in the deep fryer. Flipping once when the underside of the batter is golden.

The shrimp is done when it floats to the top and both sides of the batter is golden brown. The shrimp is a pink colour.

Baked Coconut Shrimp

This crunchy coconut shrimp is baked instead of fried,

1 pound large shrimp, peeled and deveined

1/3 cup almond flour

1 teaspoon salt

3/4 teaspoon cayenne pepper

1 cup unsweetened coconut

3 egg whites, beaten until foamy

Preheat an oven to 400 degrees F (200 degrees C). Lightly coat a baking sheet with cooking spray.

Rinse and dry shrimp with paper towels. Mix almond flour, salt, and cayenne pepper in a shallow bowl. Working with one shrimp at a time, dredge it in the almond flour mixture, then dip it in the egg white, making sure to coat the shrimp well. Then roll in the coconut, coating well. Place on the prepared baking sheet, and repeat with the remaining shrimp.

Bake the shrimp until they are bright pink on the outside and the meat is

no longer transparent in the center, and the coconut is browned. 15 to 20

minutes, flipping the shrimp halfway through.

Broiled Marinated Shrimp

16 extra large shrimp, about 1 pound, shelled and deveined

3/4 cup extra-virgin olive oil

3 garlic cloves, chopped

1/2 tsp pepper

3 lemons, cut into wedges

2 Tbsp chopped fresh rosemary or 2 tsp dried

Place shrimp on 4 long metal skewers, threading thru tails and body.

Combine oil, garlic, rosemary, and pepper in a shallow dish.

Place skewered shrimp in dish, and turn to coat well.

Marinate shrimp, turning several times, for 2 hours in refrigerator. Preheat broiler.

Set skewers on a baking sheet set 3 inches form the heat and broil shrimp, turning once, until lightly browned, and just opaque inside, about 5 minutes.

Brush with any remaining herb oil just before serving, and pass lemon wedges on the side.

Shrimp Mojo de Ajo

24 unpeeled, large raw shrimp

1/2 cup Mojo de Ajo

24 (6-inch) wooden skewers

Garnishes: lime wedges, fresh cilantro sprigs, coarse sea salt

Peel shrimp, leaving tails on; devein, if desired. Combine shrimp and Mojo

de Ajo, tossing to coat. Let stand 30 minutes.

Meanwhile, soak wooden skewers in water 30 minutes.

Remove shrimp from Mojo de Ajo, discarding marinade. Thread 1 shrimp onto

each skewer.

Grill, covered with grill lid, over medium-high heat 1 to 2 minutes on each side or just until shrimp turn pink. Garnish, if desired.

Sesame Shrimp with Cilantro-Lime Sauce

6 tablespoons white sesame seeds, toasted

1/2 cup mayonnaise

2 tablespoons finely chopped cilantro

1 tablespoon fresh lime juice

2 teaspoons coconut animos

1/2 teaspoon toasted sesame oil

1/4 teaspoon cayenne pepper

2 scallions, finely chopped (white and light green parts only)

1 pound medium uncooked shrimp (about 36), peeled and deveined

2 tablespoons vegetable oil

1/4 teaspoon kosher salt

1/8 teaspoon freshly ground black pepper

36 small metal skewers or wooden toothpicks

Heat the oven to 400°F and arrange a rack in the middle. Line a baking

sheet with foil; set aside. Place the sesame seeds on a plate; set aside.

Combine the mayonnaise, cilantro, lime juice, soy sauce, sesame oil,

cayenne pepper, and scallions in a medium bowl; set aside.

Place the shrimp in a large bowl, add the vegetable oil, salt, and pepper,

and toss to coat. Dip one side of each shrimp in the toasted sesame seeds,

skewer, and place on the prepared baking sheet, seeds-side up. Bake until the shrimp are firm to the touch, about 5 to 7 minutes. Serve immediately

with the dipping sauce.

Cilantro Pesto Shrimp

1 lb local or wild medium shrimp (21-30's- between 21 and 30 per pound)

Peeled and De-veined (P&D's if you want the lingo)

1/2 cup cilantro pesto [in Dressings Chapter]

7 x 8" wooden skewers

Soak the wooden skewers for at least 2 hours. This will help prevent them

from going up in flames when they hit the grill.

I prefer to marinate the shrimp first before skewering to keep the skewers nice n clean. Marinate the shrimp for at least 2 hours up to 6.

Once marinated, with clean hands skewer 3 shrimp on each skewer. You can of

course use larger metal skewers if you prefer. The skewers are really only

for cooking purposes so you don't end up loosing some shrimp on the grill.

On a preheated hot grill, sear each skewer for 2 minutes each side until

shrimp turn opaque and are firm to the touch.

Barbecued Calamari

750 g calamari (4 whole)

1/4 cup olive oil (60ml)

1 lemon (juice and grated rind of)

2 teaspoons dried oregano

5 garlic cloves (sliced)

1 chili (long red sliced)

To clean calamari, remove heads and tentacles by pulling gently from the bodies.

Pull intestines from calamari tubes and discard and cut tentacles away from

heads, just below the eyes.

Discard heads and pull transparent quills out of tubes and discard.

Place a little salt on your fingers for grip and peel skin from tubes and discard and then rinse tubes under cold water.

Cut tubes on one side, flatten and score inside in a criss-cross pattern

and cut into quarters lengthways.

Combine calamari, tentacles, olive oil, lemon rind and juice, oregano,

garlic and chilli in a bowl, cover and refrigerate for 2 hours or overnight

to marinate.

Preheat a barbecue plate on high and cook calamari turning for 3 to 5

minutes until browned and just opaque.

Transfer to a bowl and season to taste and serve.

Grilled Calamari

1/4 c. olive oil

1 1/2 tbsp. fresh lemon juice (1 small lemon)

1/2 tsp. coarse salt

1 clove garlic, thinly sliced

2 sprigs fresh oregano (or 1/2 tsp. dried)

1 lb. fresh squid, cleaned, rinsed, and well dried

freshly ground black pepper

In a serving bowl, whisk together the olive oil, lemon juice, and salt.

Stir in the garlic and whole oregano sprigs.

Heat a grill pan over the high heat. (Alternatively, you can cook the

squid on the grill.) When very hot, add the squid and char each side for

1 minute. Remove from the pan and slice crosswise into 1/4-inch rings,

including the tendrils. Add the squid to the lemon sauce. Crack freshly

ground pepper over and serve immediately.

Roasted Red Pepper, Garlic and Anchovy Appetizer

1 (12 ounce) jar roasted red peppers

6-12 canned anchovy fillets

finely minced garlic

extra virgin olive oil

Place roasted red peppers on plate.

Place 2-3 anchovy fillets on peppers (more if desired).

Add desired amount of minced garlic (jarred is best).

Add extra virgin oil as desired.

Black Olive Tapenade

1/2 pound pitted Kalamata olives, or other black olives

2 anchovy fillets

1 small clove garlic, peeled

2 tablespoons extra-virgin olive oil

2 tablespoons capers, drained

1 tablespoon fresh juice from 1 lemon

1 teaspoon finely chopped fresh thyme leaves

1 teaspoon whole grain Dijon mustard

Kosher salt and freshly ground black pepper

Place olives, anchovies, garlic, olive oil, capers, lemon juice, thyme, and

mustard in the workbowl of a food processor fitted with a steel blade.

Pulse until uniformly chopped into a thick paste, stopping to scrape down

sides as necessary. Season with salt and pepper to taste. Use immediately

or transfer to an airtight container and store in refrigerator for up to

two weeks.

Green Olive Tapenade

1 cup pitted green olives

5 anchovy fillets

3 tablespoons capers, drained

1 small garlic clove

2 teaspoons freshly squeezed lemon juice

Place olives, anchovies, capers, garlic, and lemon juice in the bowl of a

food processor. Pulse until a coarse paste forms. Store in an airtight

container, refrigerated, for up to 1 week.

Olive Tapenade

2 cups black olives, such as Kalamata, pitted

4 anchovy fillets

1/2 cup fresh flat-leaf parsley

1 garlic clove

2 tablespoons extra-virgin olive oil

Pulse olives, anchovies, parsley, and garlic in a food processor until

coarsely chopped. Stir in oil. Cover, and refrigerate up to 3 days.

Black Olive Paste

1 cup pitted black olives, such as Kalamata, oil-cured, or Gaeta

5 anchovy fillets

5 garlic cloves

1 tablespoon fresh rosemary leaves or 1 teaspoon dried rosemary

1/2 teaspoon freshly ground black pepper

1/2 cup virgin olive oil

In the bowl of a food processor fitted with a steel blade, blend the

olives, anchovy fillets, garlic, rosemary, and pepper to a smooth paste.

With the processor on, slowly add the olive oil until combined, about 2

minutes. Transfer the olive paste to a small bowl, and set aside.

Olive-Caper Spread

2 cups pitted brine-cured black olives

1 cup loosely packed fresh parsley leaves

2 tablespoons rinsed capers

2 anchovy fillets, optional

Finely grated zest and juice of 1 lemon

2 tablespoons olive oil

In a food processor, combine black olives (such as Kalamata), parsley

leaves, rinsed capers, and anchovy fillets (optional) with lemon zest and

juice; process until finely chopped.

Salsa Verde

1/2 cup extra-virgin olive oil

9 flat anchovy fillets, drained, patted dry, and minced

2 1/2 tablespoons drained bottled capers (preferably nonpareil), rinsed and finely chopped

6 tablespoons finely chopped fresh flat-leaf parsley

3 tablespoons finely chopped fresh mint

1 teaspoon lemon juice

1/8 teaspoon black pepper

Stir together all ingredients in a bowl.

Cooks' note: Salsa verde can be made 1 day ahead and chilled, covered.

Smoked Salmon with Mango and Coconut

1 mango, peeled, pitted, cut into cubes of 2 cm.

100 grams smoked salmon, cut into strips

1 tablespoon grated coconut

Pierce a strip of salmon and into a piece of mango. Repeat. Sprinkle

with grated coconut. Serve at room temperature.

Roasted Asparagus Wrapped in Smoked Salmon

1 pound fresh asparagus

1 tablespoon olive oil

Fresh rosemary chopped

Salt and Pepper to taste

Trim asparagus. Lay spears flat on a foil lined baking sheet. Drizzle with

olive oil and sprinkle with salt and pepper and a little fresh rosemary.

Toss asparagus around to evenly coat.

Cook in oven for 10 minutes at 400 degrees until golden brown and tender.

Wrap each spear with smoked salmon and serve.

Asparagus and Smoked Salmon Bundles

1 bunch asparagus, ends trimmed (about 20 spears)

2 tablespoons olive oil

1 tablespoon chopped fresh rosemary leaves

Pinch kosher salt

Pinch freshly ground black pepper

4 to 6 ounces thinly sliced smoked salmon (1 slice per asparagus spear)

Preheat the oven to 400 degrees F.

Lay the asparagus on a foil-lined baking sheet. Drizzle with olive oil.

Sprinkle with rosemary, salt, and pepper. Roast until cooked and starting

to brown around the edges, about 10 minutes. Remove from the oven and transfer to another baking sheet to cool.

Once the asparagus have cooled, wrap each spear in a slice of smoked

salmon. Arrange on a serving platter and serve at room temperature.

Smoked Salmon Wrapped Scallops With Pistachio Horseradish Crust

1 regular maple plank, soaked in water

1/2 cup ground pistachio nuts

3 cloves garlic, minced

2 green onions, finely chopped

1/2 cup diced cucumber

2 tbsp. prepared horseradish

2 tbsp. honey

2 tbsp. lemon juice

2 tbsp. olive oil

Sea salt and freshly ground black pepper

12 jumbo scallops (the biggest, and most similar in size you can find)

12 slices smoked salmon

In a bowl, mix together the pistachio nuts, garlic, green onions, cucumber, horseradish, honey, lemon juice and olive oil. Season with salt and pepper to taste.

Using a paper towel, pat the scallops dry and then season with salt and pepper. Wrap a slice of smoked salmon around each scallop and secure with a toothpick. Crust the topside of the scallop generously with the pistachio mixture.

Preheat the grill to high heat, 500-550°F. Place plank on grill and close lid. Heat the wood for 3 to 5 minutes, until it crackles and smokes. Open the grill and place the scallops, crust side up, on the plank, spaced about 1/2" apart. Close the lid and bake for 6 to 8 minutes, until the scallops are golden brown and the crust crispy.

Shrimp Salmon Rumaki with Dill Mayonnaise

12 cooked shrimp

12 canned water chestnuts

12 thin strips smoked salmon

lemon juice

freshly ground pepper

Wrap shrimp around water chestnut. Wrap salmon strip around shrimp and

chestnut. Secure with toothpick. Sprinkle with lemon juice and freshly

ground pepper. Serve with Dill Mayonnaise.

Smoked Salmon with Mango and Coconut

1 mango, peeled, pitted, cut into cubes of 2 cm.

100 grams smoked salmon, cut into strips

1 tablespoon grated coconut

Pierce a strip of salmon and into a piece of mango. Repeat. Sprinkle

with grated coconut. Serve at room temperature.

Roasted Asparagus Wrapped in Smoked Salmon

1 pound fresh asparagus

1 tablespoon olive oil

Fresh rosemary chopped

Salt and Pepper to taste

Trim asparagus. Lay spears flat on a foil lined baking sheet. Drizzle with

olive oil and sprinkle with salt and pepper and a little fresh rosemary.

Toss asparagus around to evenly coat.

Cook in oven for 10 minutes at 400 degrees until golden brown and tender.

Wrap each spear with smoked salmon and serve.

Asparagus and Smoked Salmon Bundles

1 bunch asparagus, ends trimmed (about 20 spears)

2 tablespoons olive oil

1 tablespoon chopped fresh rosemary leaves

Pinch kosher salt

Pinch freshly ground black pepper

4 to 6 ounces thinly sliced smoked salmon (1 slice per asparagus spear)

Preheat the oven to 400 degrees F.

Lay the asparagus on a foil-lined baking sheet. Drizzle with olive oil.

Sprinkle with rosemary, salt, and pepper. Roast until cooked and starting

to brown around the edges, about 10 minutes. Remove from the oven and

transfer to another baking sheet to cool.

Once the asparagus have cooled, wrap each spear in a slice of smoked

salmon.

Arrange on a serving platter and serve at room temperature.

Smoked Salmon Wrapped Scallops With Pistachio Horseradish Crust

1 regular maple plank, soaked in water

1/2 cup ground pistachio nuts

3 cloves garlic, minced

2 green onions, finely chopped

1/2 cup diced cucumber

2 tbsp. prepared horseradish

2 tbsp. honey

2 tbsp. lemon juice

2 tbsp. olive oil

Sea salt and freshly ground black pepper

12 jumbo scallops (the biggest, and most similar in size you can find)

12 slices smoked salmon

In a bowl, mix together the pistachio nuts, garlic, green onions, cucumber,

horseradish, honey, lemon juice and olive oil. Season with salt and pepper

to taste.

Using a paper towel, pat the scallops dry and then season with salt and

pepper. Wrap a slice of smoked salmon around each scallop and secure with a

toothpick. Crust the topside of the scallop generously with the pistachio

mixture.

Preheat the grill to high heat, 500-550°F. Place plank on grill and close

lid. Heat the wood for 3 to 5 minutes, until it crackles and smokes. Open

the grill and place the scallops, crust side up, on the plank, spaced about

1/2" apart. Close the lid and bake for 6 to 8 minutes, until the scallops

are golden brown and the crust crispy.

Shrimp Salmon Rumaki with Dill Mayonnaise

12 cooked shrimp

12 canned water chestnuts

12 thin strips smoked salmon

lemon juice

freshly ground pepper

Wrap shrimp around water chestnut. Wrap salmon strip around shrimp and

chestnut. Secure with toothpick. Sprinkle with lemon juice and freshly

ground pepper. Serve with Dill Mayonnaise.

Tuna Salad Bites

1 (6-ounce) can chunk white tuna in water, drained

1/2 cup finely chopped carrot

1/3 cup thinly sliced green onions

1/4 cup sliced pimiento-stuffed olives

1/4 cup mayonnaise

3 tablespoons minced fresh parsley

1 tablespoon lemon juice

1/2 teaspoon black pepper

2 medium cucumbers, cut into 1/2-inch slices

Combine first 8 ingredients in a medium bowl, stirring well. Cover and chill

at least 1 hour.

Scoop out a hollow space in center of one side of each cucumber slice, using a 1/2-teaspoon circular measuring spoon or a small melon baller. Fill

centers of cucumber slices with tuna mixture.

Serve immediately.

Tuna Tartare

1 pound sushi grade tuna, finely diced

3 tablespoons olive oil

1/4 teaspoon wasabi powder

1 tablespoon sesame seeds

1/8 teaspoon cracked black pepper

In a bowl, stir together olive oil, wasabi powder, sesame seeds, and

cracked black pepper. Toss tuna into mixture until evenly coated. Adjust

seasoning as desired with additional wasabi powder or black pepper.

Asian Tuna Tartare

1/4 cup paleo oil [like macadamia oil]

2 teaspoons grated fresh ginger

1 pound sushi-grade tuna

1/4 cup finely chopped cilantro

1 teaspoon minced jalapeño

1 1/2 teaspoons wasabi powder

1 teaspoon toasted sesame seeds

1 tablespoon finely chopped scallion

1 1/2 tablespoons lemon juice, plus half a lemon

Sea salt and freshly ground pepper

1 tomato: peeled, seeded and cut into 1/8-inch dice

In a bowl, combine the corn oil and ginger and let stand at room temperature for at least 2 hours. Strain the oil.

With a very sharp knife, cut the tuna into 1/8-inch dice. In a large bowl,

combine the tuna with 3 tablespoons of the ginger oil, 3 tablespoons of the

cilantro and the jalapeño, wasabi, sesame seeds, scallion and lemon juice.

Mix gently and season with salt and pepper.

Stand a 1 1/2-inch-tall and 2 1/4-inch-round mold or a biscuit cutter in

the center of a salad plate. Fill the mold with tuna tartare, pressing

gently. Lift off the mold. Repeat with the remaining tartare.

Drizzle the remaining ginger oil around each tartare and sprinkle with the

tomato, the remaining tablespoon of cilantro and a squeeze of lemon juice.

Serve immediately.

Tuna Tartare Sicilian-Style

1 lb tuna or yellowtail

2 T extra-virgin olive oil

1 T tiny capers

1 T finely chopped shallot

1 T finely chopped Sicilian green olives

1/2 t. red pepper flakes, or 1 small chile pepper, chopped fine

1 t pine nuts, toasted and chopped

1 lemon, quartered

2 T fennel fronds, for garnish

Salt and freshly ground black pepper to taste

Chop the tuna into very small dice, about 1/4 inch. Use a very sharp knife.

Mix with the olive oil, capers, shallot, chile pepper, pine nuts and

olives, then season with salt and pepper to taste.

Garnish with the fennel fronds and serve with a lemon wedge.

Conclusion

Thank you again for downloading this book! I hope this book was able to help you to get started in cooking healthy Chinese dishes. Cooking Chinese dishes can be quite satisfying and time saving. So, do get your ingredients and equipments ready and start cooking!

Please check out my other books in this series:

Part 2

CEDAR KEY CRAB BISQUE

INGREDIENTS

4 TABLESPOONS BUTTER

WHOLE SPRING ONION CUT INTO THIN SLICES

1/2 JAR ROASTED RED BELL PEPPERS CHOPPED IN TINY PIECES

3 TABLESPOONS FLOUR

3 CUPS HALF & HALF

8 OUNCES CRAB MEAT

4 TABLESPOONS BUTTER

SALT & PEPPER TO TASTE

3 TABLESPOONS CREAM SHERRY

PARSLEY AND PAPRIKA

METHOD

Melt 2 tablespoons butter in a sauce pan; sauté the onion and pepper. Add the flour to the butter to make a roux. Cook slowly, about 3 minutes so the flour will lose its flat taste. Add a little half & half to make the roux.

In a pot, heat the remaining half & half; then add the roux, parsley, paprika, and crabmeat to the pot. Cook until hot. Remove from heat and add the sherry and remaining butter. Place in serving bowls and garnish with chopped parsley, spring onion and paprika. Now you can taste Cedar Key cooking.

WHAT HAPPENED TO ELDORA?

In the year 1877, the Indian wars in Florida had ended. Two families started a settlement near Turtle Mound. In later years Turtle Mound was deemed a state archeological historical Indian site. The location is just south of New Smyrna Beach, not far from the inlet.

The two families brought in building supplies by paddle wheel ferry to an area called Oak Grove. They built two large two-story houses complete with widow's walks. They also built a boathouse for a 20-foot boat or more. The homestead was called Eldora, after the two sisters Ellen and Dora Pitzer. They were pictured in long black dresses and high button shoes in a family album that was mysteriously left behind.

Sometime prior to the late 1950s, the old boathouse had been turned into a small restaurant. The plinki-tinki sounds of the old upright piano played by 'Curly' made the beer taste even better. Eldora lived again! Clientele came from all over Florida and South Georgia for the fishing and the food. Many prominent sports people and politicians flocked to the little restaurant. The restaurant served buckets of tasty oysters on the half shell. Positioned over the water, the patrons would toss the oyster shells out of the open windows into the river. This was casual dining at its best. Crab cake, shrimp and oyster sandwiches were also served. Eating and drinking at El Dora was just plain fun. One black day, the restaurant mysteriously burnt to the ground ending an era.

The restaurant was rebuilt of concrete blocks, but never recovered. Later, the original boathouse iron door latch was found in the Indian River waters and presented to Judge Lon Cornelius on a plaque which graces a wall in the Cornelius home at New Smyrna Beach. It is a reminder of the good times at El Dora.

In the late 1980s one of the houses was destroyed by fire. The state fenced of the remaining house for several years and then they rebuilt the last house as an historical site. It is known as the State House at El Dora. It looks a lot like the original but not the same. Now you can restore the famous El Dora crab cake, like the ones served at the once famous El Dora Boathouse Restaurant.

EL DORA CRAB CAKES

The Last Original House at Eldora: Much Different from the "Restored" House

INGREDIENTS

ONE POUND CRABMEAT

1/4 CUP MINCED CELERY

1/4 CUP MINCED ONION

1/4 CUP MINCED RED BELL PEPPER

1 TEASPOON CHOPPED PARSLEY

1-1/2 TEASPOON THYME

1 TEASPOON GRANULATED GARLIC

1 TEASPOON OREGANO

1 TEASPOON POWDERED MUSTARD

3 TABLESPOONS OLIVE OIL + ¼ CUP FOR FRYING

1/2 + 1 CUP BREAD CRUMBS OR 6 SALTINE CRACKERS, CRUMBLED

1 EGG

SALT AND PEPPER

METHOD

Sauté the vegetables in 3 tablespoons olive oil and cool to room temperature.

Beat the egg into the ½ cup bread crumbs. Add the vegetables and crabmeat, mix, form into patties. Roll the patties in 1 cup bread crumbs and sauté in the remaining oil

J.B.'S FISH CAMP 1960s–2008

South of New Smyrna Beach, Florida, on the Indian River, (just across the street from the beach) there once was a small fish camp with a crab corral and a crab steamer inside the shack. They kept live crabs in the concrete corral to provide enough crabs for their clientele. The crabs were steamed whole, and soon became a Mecca for both the beach crowd and anglers fishing the Indian River. People would gather around the 5 or 6 tables inside the screened-in crab shack to drink pitchers of beer, crack and eat crabs by the dozen. Two such people, known as "Dude Boy" and "Fat Rat" spent a lot of good times eating crabs and drinking beer here. However, as time went by, progress made its changes.

Gone are the crab corrals, screened-in shack with the half dozen tables and prominent crab steamer. Gone are the newspaper covered tables and rickety chairs. However, the good times and the boat ramp are still there, the dock much improved, and the small square crab shack with the crab steamer was replaced by a much larger restaurant.

Today, the site is occupied by the Capt. J. B's Fish Camp Seafood Restaurant. Their motto is, "Southern

Seafood with an Attitude". Both indoor and outdoor casual dining is offered with a much more varied and sophisticated seafood menu. The view of the Indian River is the center piece of the outside dining area. Casual seafood dining at its best. Oh yes, Dude Boy and Fat Rat still occasionally eat seafood and drink beer there. Let the good times roll.

NEW SYMRNA BEACH CRAB IMPERIAL

INGREDIENTS (SERVES 4)

1 POUND CRAB MEAT

1/4 CUP MAYONAISE

2 TABLESPOONS BUTTER

1 TEASPOON DRY MUSTARD

1 EGG

1 TEASPOON MINCED GREEN BELL PEPPER

1 TEASPOON MINCED RED BELL PEPPER

1 TEASPOON MINCED CELERY

1 TEASPOON MINCED ONION

1/2 TEASPOON LEA & PERRINS WORCESTERSHIRE SAUCE

1 TABLESPOON SHERRY

1 TEASPOON THYME

1 TEASPOON LEMON JUICE

GRATED SHARP CHEDDAR CHEESE TO COVER EACH MAMEKIN PLUS A DASH OF PAPRIKA

METHOD

Sauté veggies, 6 thru 9, in 2 tablespoons butter until done; let cool. In a bowl, beat the egg and add the lemon juice, mustard, veggies, Worcestershire, thyme, sherry and crab meat. Spoon the mixture into ramekins or crab shells, top with mayo, cheese & paprika. Bake in oven at 350 until set.

THE PIRATE GHOST

Back when the world was young, only sails and brave men propelled ships across the seas. Savannah, Georgia was a major port of call for these ships and a haven for both sailors of good repute and pirates. There was a house up the hill from the riverfront. The house served food and drink. Pirates had a secret tunnel from the house to the docks to elude would be captors. Hence, the name 'Pirates House" became a legend.

Rumor has it that there was a particularly mean pirate; an Englishman called Big Bellied Bob. Bob loved She-Crab soup. When in port, he demanded gallons of the wonderful elixir. Big Bellied bob not only frequented the Pirates House, but also a nearby brothel.

Unfortunately, Bob was not a nice pirate. He beat the girls who attended him unmercifully. He also expected the girls to trek the streets all hours of the night to acquire more She-Crab soup.

One night, after a lot of rum and a mean temper, he demanded more soup. Two of the girls ran down to the Pirates House and came back with a steaming pot of the "Pirate Houses Best She-Crab soup". However, this time it was laced with poison. Bob swore a Pirates oath to get even with the girls.

The actual brothel house still stands today. It has been reworked and made into a posh three-story apartment house. To this day, the house is considered haunted by the ghost of Big Bellied Bob. Mysterious happenings are blamed on the ghost. Missing keys, later found in another apartment, bathrobes hung on the bathroom door somehow may show up in the parking lot. Those living in the apartment building believe Big Bellied Bob is responsible. After a rash of incidents, a bowl of She-Crab soup is left out on the table, and often disappears after midnight.

The Pirates House has been a renowned restaurant in Savannah for many years now and is a delight to see. The food and service are always excellent. Never go to

Savannah without taking at least one meal at the Pirates House.

From an Old Painting

Could This Be Big Bellied Bob?

SAVANNAH SHE-CRAB SOUP

Note: the original recipe included eggs from the female crab. Since it is illegal to take crags with eggs attached, chicken egg yolks are substituted. The difference is barely noticeable.

INGREDIENTS

2 POUNDS BLUE CRAB

1 QUART HALF & HALF

1-1/2 LEMONS, JUICED

1/4 CUP SHERRY WINE

1 TEASPOON PEPPER

1 TEASPOON SALT

1 TEASPOON NUTMEG

1 MED.ONION, MINCED

1/2 STALK CELERY, MINCED

3 EGG YOKES

2 TABLESPOONS FLOU

2 TABLESPOONS BUTTER

METHOD

In a heavy pot, melt the butter and sauté the celery and onions until clear; without burning the butter. Add the flour and cook about 3 minutes over a medium heat. Pour in half of the Half & Half into the roux with the veggies. In the remaining half of the Half & Half, beat the egg yolks and add the mixture to the pot. Add the sherry, lemon, salt, pepper and nutmeg. Bring the mixture to a near boil until it thickens. Set the pot off the stove and add the crabmeat. Let it stand 5 minutes before serving. (The crab will be cooked.) Garnish with chopped parsley and paprika.

FISH

THE HURRICANE OF 1922

"In those days, a fish diner in the form of grits and grunts was a staple for the construction crews on the railroad. A grunt is a pan fish that is found on most any bottom that holds baitfish. On occasion, we'd be fortunate enough to acquire Yellowtail Snapper. Yellowtail Snapper are found on the coral reefs and are excellent table fare. They are found in schools and are best caught at night using chum to bring them to the surface. When it comes to eating, Yellowtail Snapper can't be beat. However, how they are prepared makes a world of difference" he said.

"When the hurricane of 1922 hit our railroad construction site, we huddled in one corner of our dormitory shack. The roof lifted and turned but did not blow completely off. Others at the site were not so lucky.

One group was assigned to guard the supplies during the blow. While on guard, two men were blown off the island by winds of over a hundred miles per hour. They survived by desperately clinging to a railroad tie. The men floated for several days. The Gulf Stream pushed them North, up the coastline of Florida. They were near death when finally rescued off Palm Beach. I doubt they ever ate grits and grunts again.

After the hurricane, I left the railroad job and found some tomato farm land in the everglades. That way, I could tell which was the low lands with water standing and avoid those areas. One year I met a band of Indians camped in my Tomato Field, which turned out to be very fortunate for me. But that's another story. I still like a good yellowtail snapper any way it's fixed."

GRILLED YELLOWTAIL SNAPPER

INGREDIENTS (SERVES 2)

2 WHOLE YELLOW TAIL SNAPPER

1/2 LEMON PER FILET

OLIVE OIL

SALT & PEPPER

1 MANGO, DICED OR CHOPPED

AN EQUAL AMOUNT OF CHUNKY MILD OR MEDIUM SALSA

METHOD

Use the whole fish, cleaned. With a sharp knife, score each side of the fish with evenly spaced diagonal cuts,

4 or five times down to the bone. Rub the fish inside and out with the lemon juice, then salt and pepper. Let stand 5 minutes or so. Coat the fish with olive oil to keep it from burning. Grill over medium heat and turn so it cooks evenly and completely through.

Mix the mango and the salsa in even amounts. Serve with the fish and a crisp salad.

FISHING THE F.I.T.O.A.

THE F.I.T.O.A. (Fishing Is The Only Answer)

The only lunch on the FITOA was a package of bologna, a loaf of bread and a jar of mayonnaise. It was good if you liked bologna. There were good days and bad days. Once, we hooked two sailfish at the same time. On another trip nine sailfish were hooked slow trolling live mullet. On a Mako tournament out of the Sailfish Marina, the winds blew 25 to 30 mph. Only one other boat fished. The FITOA's radio mike was jammed in the open position, broadcasting short tempers and 4 letter words to the entire East Coast

One cold winter day out of Jupiter, the FIOA took a breaking wave, drenching the whole crew. Then the steering broke. The crew jockeyed the motor with a rope tied to the motor. The boat and crew ended up tired and wet on a Jupiter sand bar.

The worst day the FITOA had was when she took a 20-foot wave over the bow and swamped. Surfers rescued the anglers, but Randy stayed with the boat until it was beached. The FITOA was dragged across the beach, brought home and reconditioned including a new motor and still fishes as this book is printed.

One summer day fishing out of the Ocean Reef Club on Key Largo, several dolphin fish (mahi-mahi) were boated. That night, Randy unveiled a baked dolphin dish like you have never tasted before. However, the recipe that Randy started in 1976 in the Florida Key's, has spread like wildfire ever since. You may have already tasted it, if not, now you can.

MAHI-MAHI FITOA STYLE

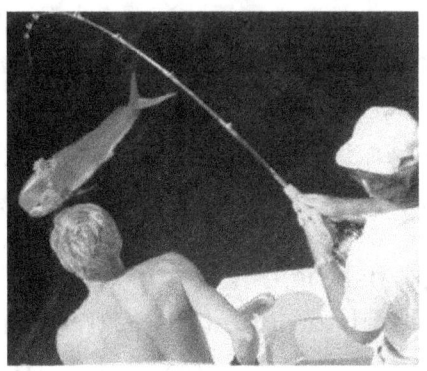

Catching a Dophin Fish (Mahi-Mahi)

INGREDIENTS

ONE DOLPHIN FILET (MAHI-MAHI); OR OTHER FIRM FLESHED FISH. LIKE KINGFISH, MACKEREL WAHOO, GROUPER ETC.

A BAKING SHEET TO MATCH THE FILET

ONE LEMON CUT IN HALF

MAYONAISE

PAPRIKA

COARSE BREAD CRUMBS

METHOD

Place the filet skin side down (it does not have to be skinned) on the baking sheet. Squeeze the juice of one lemon over the filet and let it stand 5 minutes. Cover the filet with mayonnaise (not salad dressing). Sprinkle paprika, salt and pepper over the mayonnaise. Cover the whole thing with coarse bread crumbs, (Japanese Panko bread crumbs are the best). Bake for roughly 20 minutes until the bread crumbs begin to brown. This may be the best fish you ever tasted.

RED SNAPPER FISHING: 1803–2008

The crews of snapper schooners in the 1800s always had a captain, a cook and a lead-man in addition to the rest of the crew. The lead man was a key player, and the crew often took turns throwing the lead. The lead was used to find hard bottom. This was prevalent up into the 1950s for the grouper boats out of Tarpon Springs, Florida. The lead had a hollow lower end, which contained a mixture of soap and wax. This was to get bottom debris to stick to it. Live coral or small creatures indicated live bottom and possible fish. On snapper schooners, the lead line usually had one or 2 baited hooks attached to it. When snapper was indicated or taken on the lead line, the crew went into action.

The dory's (small boat) were launched if the indications were good enough to cover more area. The cooks only other job was to take the wheel while the crew caught fish. Grouper and Porgy were also taken, but these were not the primary target. Porgy (a very good eating fish) was often not kept at all; only red snapper.

Most schooners had bunkers in the hole to keep the blocks of ice for the catch. The crew used hand-lines with a rag wrapped around one hand to fight the fish with. Catches were recorded up to 1500 fish taken on a trip. There were always fish to catch; they just had to find them.[1]

Today, modern individual ships with electronic GPS global positioning devices and Sonar fish finders have made the job much easier; too easy in some respects.

Modern methods, including long lines and fish traps currently take their toll, resulting in regulation to curb over-fishing. Shrimp trawlers catch and kill tons of juvenile snapper in their nets as by-catch. Alternative methods of sustaining the fish stocks are constantly being re-visited by the federal bureaucracy, which tends to lean towards the commercial interest. However, the recreational catch of grouper and snapper is many times the value of the commercial catch. The politics of the snapper-grouper fishery is a sham. Good management would solve this continuous debacle. The dollar value of the recreational fishery when all factors are taken into account such as: boat sales, lodging, food, drink, bait, fuel, guides, and other miscellaneous jobs is monumental. Florida benefits greatly from recreational fishing but is treated by the "fed" as the stepchild due to lopsided politics.

LEMON STUFFED FISH

INGREDIENTS

3 TO 5 POUND SNAPPER, GROUPER, SEA BASS or OTHER GOOD FISH

1/2 CUP CHOPPED CELEARY

2 LEMONS, ZEST GRATED OFF, PEELED & CUBED

1/2 CUP CHOPPED ONION

4 CUPS SEASONED CROUTONS

1 TEASPOON PAPRIKA

3/4 CUP SOUR CREAM

1/2 TEASPOON SALT

OLIVE OIL

3 TO 4 STRIPS BACON

METHOD

Place the celery and onion in a tiny bit of olive oil and sauté. Place in a large mixing bowl. Add all other ingredients to the bowl. Split the fish from the bottom, cutting both sides of the backbone up to the dorsal fin, but not through. Remove the backbone. This leaves the top of the fish connected. Lay the fish open (like a book). Cover he bottom portion with stuffing, about 2 inches thick. Fold the other side of the fish over the stuffing. Wrap each fish (if more than 1) with 3 or 4 strips of bacon, depending upon the size of the fish. Lay the completed fish in a baking dish or pan. Bake at 350 until the bacon is crisp. Spoon the drippings over the fish. Serve

Baked Redfish with Lemon Stuffing

TARPON SPRINGS 1961

"We rented a house at Anclote village near Tarpon Springs and shared expenses with Jim Lee and Marko King in Anclote village. The house was only block from Tacy's Fish Camp on the Anclote River. It was just a stone's throw from the Gulf of Mexico. For a $2.00 bill, we could buy a bucket of crabs or shrimp from the folks at Tacy's. Later on, Tacy's was sold and became Duke's fish camp and is now a high and dry marina. But back in the 1960s, we caught grouper and sold them for .10 cents a pound. Tarpon Springs was a town of 5,000, most of whom were Greek. We enjoyed the town's people and grouper fishing in the Gulf.

One warm summer day, a French tourist was admiring our catch of grouper at the dock. He said he had never caught a fish as big. We talked and eventually we invited him to go fishing. He had a great time catching 12 to 14-pound grouper. He said he had never enjoyed anything so much and wanted to return the favor. He asked if he could give Jim a great grouper recipe (Jim was our cook) Marko did the dishes and I kept the house clean. We all said we could fry grouper as good as anyone, but he insisted. He said the fish would not be fried, but we would like it anyway. Well, I doubted that! Jim either fried or boiled everything we ate. But we kept an open mind. Jim took the recipe but asked "Frenchie" to come to our house and give him a lesson. He did, and we gathered the ingredients, and he proceeded to cook up slabs of grouper the likes of which we had never tasted before.

Frenchie started to cook and said. "I'm gonna Waller this fish in egg and flour, then sauté 'em in sweet luscious butter," he said a mocking southern drawl with a French accent. "Then I'll cover them with a lemony wine sauce and topped off with chopped walnuts. He fixed a side dish of sautéed green grapes. I call this a" palate pleaser" Frenchie said. He threatened to smack me with the spatula if I ate any of the grapes. Chomping on a grape between bites made each bite of fish taste like the first bite all over again." You should really try this one although, I still like my grouper fried" Chuck remarked.

Oh yes, I learned to cook the dish and subsequently left to go back to school, leaving Chuck and Marko in Tarpon Springs. Marko moved to California and Chuck married Sharon, a local girl. They have a family, a house with a garage so full you can't see from one side to the other, a dog, and chickens that lay eggs in his boat. Life was good, and I moved back to Tarpon Springs so Chuck and I could fish together more often."

Chuck died December 10, 1998. He is survived by his wife, Sharon, children, Mark and Melissa, and by the grandchildren, Megan, Michael, Sawyer, Ryan and Alec; so far! (And by his friends). Chuck loved to catch grouper. If his grouper wasn't fried, he didn't have much use for it; or any other fish for that matter. However, this recipe is dedicated to him anyway.

TAMPA BAY FILET

INGREDIENTS (SERVES 2)

TWO HAND SIZE FILETS OF ANY GOOD FISH

1 CUP FLOUR, SEASONED WITH S & P

1 EGG, BEATEN INO 1/2 CUP MILK

3/4 CUP FRUITY WHITE WINE

1/2 LEMON JUICED

1 STICK BUTTER

1 1/2 CUP GREEN GRAPES

1/4 CUP CHOPPED WALNUTS

METHOD

Heat a pan with ½ stick butter.

Dredge the filets in the flour first, then the egg wash, (which is normally backwards) but will create an absorbing coating purposely.

Sauté the filets in the hot butter pan, being carefully not to burn the butter.

Set the fish on the serving plates.

Place the green grapes into the pan and cook until they begin to turn color.

Set the grapes next to the fish.

Add the lemon juice to the wine, turn the heat up, adding a little more butter and flour, making a thick white sauce (roux).

Add the lemon juice to the wine and pour into the pan with the roux.

Stir the mixture into a thin wine sauce.

Pour the wine sauce over the grapes and fish filets. Top with Walnuts.

Fat Rat and Dude Boy with Two Grouper

THE OLD BAIT HOUSE

In the old days, back in 1980 or so, a new way to prepare a staple species of fish evolved. There was a tiny bait house on the eastern end of John's Pass Marina on the Treasure Island side. A very pleasant woman who was originally from Switzerland operated the bait house. Her teenage son often caught mullet off the dock with his cast net. He would sell them, still flopping on the dock to tourist and locals passing by.

Mullet are the most common fish on the planet, as they are worldwide. In Florida, there are two common mullets, the black aka striped and the white aka silver mullet. Black mullet spawn offshore but come inshore to grow up. When ready to spawn, the gather in estuaries before moving offshore and are full of eggs called "roe". Mullet almost reached a critical point in numbers in Florida but were saved by the banning of gill net fishing in Florida waters. Mullet are the fish you will see leaping out of the water in creeks, canals and around grass flats.

Since mullet, like bluefish is a very oily fish, it must be cleaned and eaten while fresh. If not, it takes on an oily taste. Because of this some folks consider mullet poor table fare. However, cooked fresh, it is a delight. Since Lon Cornelius and I had a boat in dry storage at John's

Pass Marina, I was often at the bait house. One day while walking past the bait house, I saw about a dozen freshly caught mullet flopping on the dock. I bought 6 of them from the teenage son. While he was bagging them for me, the very pleasant owner of the bait house asked me how I intended to prepare the fish.

In the South, mullet is usually smoked or rolled in cornmeal and fried. To smoke them, they are cleaned, then split from the belly up and opened flat, but not scaled. Then they would be covered with a proprietary blend of seasonings and smoked either the hot method, or cold method. The old school anglers, would scale, clean and split the fish in two pieces, roll them in corn meal and fry them quickly (skin on). Others would filet the fish (skin off) and do the same. I told her I intended to filet and corn meal the fish then fry them.

Well, the sweet lady from Switzerland offered me a Swiss alternative. This method actually brings mullet up to the par of mangrove snapper or other better fish. I call this method "Back Bay Sauté. I use this method today on mullet, mackerel, bluefish or king mackerel for a sweeter, more flavorful taste.

BACK BAY SAUTE'

INGREDIENTS

MULLET FILETS WITH THE SKIN OFF AND RIB CAGE REMOVED

(ANY OILY FISH LIKE BLUEFISH OR MACKEREL AND KINGFISH ALSO WORK WELL WITH THIS RECIPE)

1/2 CUP FLOUR

1/4 TEASPOON SALT

1/2 TEASPOON GARLIC POWDER (GRANULATED GARLIC IS BEST)

1/2 TEASPOON THYME

METHOD

Mix all the dry ingredients together. Moisten the fish and dust in the mixture. Sauté the dusted filets in a little olive oil, to a golden brown.

The taste will amaze you, as the combination of spices will change any oily fish such as mullet, mackerel, bluefish or others to a delightful eating experience.

TASTES LIKE CHICKEN

Living with a man who refuses to eat fish can force a lady fish lover to use extreme methods; including a little white lie or two. After doing without fish for two years, I decided to fight back in a devious way. This was truly a clandestine operation. It required my best diversionary skills. I waived a chicken around in the kitchen so he would be sure to see it. Then I shaped two nice grouper filets like chicken breasts.

"Look honey, this chicken has a huge breast." I got a "wonderful" out of him, as I prepared the rest of the recipe. "This recipe is so good you won't even recognize this bird." I said. "Wait until you taste this dish (fish) I mumbled.

This dish is served with mushrooms, red bell pepper, bacon and sour cream sauce covering the patty of pork sausage and stove top dressing on top of the big grouper filet.

We sat down to dinner and my husband loved it. He lapped it all up. "This is just great darling; I do like it very much. I could barely tell it was fish, could we have real chicken tomorrow night?" He said sweetly.

This is one of two recipes in this collection that you cook for those that really don't normally have a taste for fish. They are guaranteed to like either one.

Clarence White & Jim Lee with Two Nice Grouper

CLEARWATER GROUPER SUPREME

INGREDIENTS (SERVES 2)

TWO THICK HAND SIZE GROUPER FILETS, SNAPPER OR MAHI-MAHI

1/2 BOX STOVE TOP STUFFING

1/3 POUND MILD OR HOT PORK SAUSAGE

1 8-OUNCE CONTAINER OF SOUR CREAM

1 CAN CREAM OF MUSHROOM SOUP (NOT GOLDEN)

6 SLICED MUSHROOMS

2 SLICES BACON

1/2 RED BELL PEPPER, MINCED FINE, FOR COLOR

METHOD

Make the stove top stuffing and mix with the pork sausage. Form a patty to fit on top of each filet. Wrap a bacon strip around each sausage/stuffing patty. Fasten with a toothpick or meat string. Place the fish with the patties on top in a baking dish and bake until the bacon is done. While baking, put the soup, mushrooms and sour cream in a pot.

Do not add water. Heat until warm and mix well. Ten minutes before serving, pour the mushroom sauce over the patty and filets. Mix the juices and baste the fish/patty. This is a melding of flavors that you just can't get enough of.

This is a prize-winning recipe originally made with chicken and works equally well with fish.

THE RIVER MONSTER

The Hillsborough River in the Tampa Bay Area is a hot spot for not only big garfish, but big bass, speckled perch, bluegill and warmouth perch. The original story was told by Dee Brown's parents.

At nine years old, Dee brown dreamed of catching a huge river garfish. Dee and his parents were on an expedition to look for that huge saw-toothed river monster. Their 18-foot boat glided down the river, past towering cypress trees, turtles and alligators. They set up in a shady curve of the river and began to fish. From the corner of her eye, Dee's mother saw the float as the fish pulled it under the dark river waters. She handed the rod to Dee and told him to count to 100 before striking the fish. At the end of the count, the fish had ended his run and had turned the big shiner baitfish around in his mouth, so it would go down head first. Dee looked at his mom with determination in his eyes and struck the great fish.

Startled, the huge fish leaped out of the water and the fight began. Dee held on as his father had instructed. "Don't worry dad" he said with confidence in his voice. The little rod bent double as the fish peeled off more line. At last, the youngster brought the fish to the boat. It was the largest fish he had ever seen. Dee's parents, realizing the importance of the catch to their son, had the fish mounted.

The needle nose gar-pike are caught from the Carolinas to Florida. Garfish have a pure bone white meat when cooked. As fish go, the meat is a little tougher than other fish, but extremely mild. It flakes well and is great for soups and any recipe that calls for flaked fish. It is a difficult fish to clean, as it is prehistoric in nature, with a shell of rock hard scales. A pair of scissor-like tin snips is the common tool to cut through the tough shell to get to the meat. However, the effort is worth the trouble for some.

TAMPA SWEET PEPPER PASTRY

Another really sweet recipe even non-fish lovers will love to eat

INGREDIENTS (SERVES 3)

1/2 POUND GARFISH, BLACK SEABASS, GROUPER, ANY GOOD

WHITEFISH, BAY SCALLOPS OR SHRIMP

1 SWEET BELL PEPPER, COARSLY CHOPPED

1/2 CUP CHICKEN BROTH

1/2 CUP SOUR CREAM

1/2 CUP CREAM SHERRY WINE

1/2 CUP HEAVY WHIPPING CREAM

4 MUSHROOMS, SLICED

1/2 CUP ONION COARSLEY CHOPPED

3 EACH PUFF PASTRY SHELLS, BAKED AND KEPT WARM.

4 TABLESPOONS BUTTER

METHOD

Sauté or steam the fish, flake and set it aside.

In a skillet, sauté the red bell pepper to about half done.

Add the mushrooms and onion, sauté until done.

Remove from heat and set aside.

In another sauce pan, cook the sherry down to ½ and add to the vegetables. Then cook the chicken broth down to ½ and add that to the vegetables.

Beat the egg in the cream and heat the heavy cream. Add to the veggie mix. Add the fish and mix with all the other ingredients.

Spoon the mixture into the open baked shells (let some spill over as the shells do not hold very much. Place the top crust back on. Garnish with greenery.

Serve with a salad and a side dish

HERNANDO BEACH SHARK ATTACK

The angry 8-foot hooked bull shark headed straight for the boat. Larry reeled frantically but couldn't gain line fast enough. The motor was in gear, moving the boat slowly forward.

The boat lurched, knocking Larry to the deck. The captain yelled down from the fly-bridge. "Your shark just rammed the boat. Hear he comes again." The captain shouted excitedly. This time the shark charged the whirling prop and attempted to grab it with his teeth. The boat shuttered and the shark, cut and bleeding, sank to the bottom. "Good grief" Larry exclaimed, a bit shaken, I've never seen an enraged shark before, and I hope I never see another one.

The captain moved the boat west a couple miles. They anchored up and Larry resumed grouper fishing Larry was leaning over the side so he could pull in the chum box and refill it, when the captain shouted "Here comes another shark." Larry was perched on the gunwale and was startled at the captain's excited shout. Larry promptly fell overboard. Fearing the new shark was another "enraged" bull shark. Larry clawed, scrambled and willed his way up the side and over the gunwale into the boat. Lying on the deck, wet and out of breath, he heard the captain start to laugh. "It was only a big cobia." the captain said as he came down off the fly-bridge still laughing.

Anger surged in Larry and he saw the cobia swimming close to the boat. He grabbed the 6-foot gaff hook and immediately gaffed a 60-pound fish. A 60-pound cobia is a formidable adversary. Before he could get a good grip, the fish almost pulled Larry overboard again. The captain jumped in to help and together they managed to pull the fish into the boat. The thrashing fish beat both the angler and the captain several times with the gaff hook. Bruised and out of breath, Larry who was much calmer now, awarded the fish to the captain. Later, the captain told the story to friends over a martini, inspiring the recipe for Cobia Vermouth. Now you can experience the "pork chop of the sea."

HERNANDO COBIA VERMOUTH

INGREDIENTS (SERVES 4)

4 EACH 3/8" COBIA STEAKS (ANY GOOD FIRM FISH WILL WORK)

1/2 STICK BUTTER

1/2 CUP FLOUR, SEASONED WITH SALT & PEPPER

2 TABLESPOONS SMALL CAPERS

1/2 TEASPOON SALT

1/2 CUP DRY VERMOUTH

PEPPER TO TASTE

LEMON JUICE

METHOD

Cut the cobia, kingfish, or mackerel into steaks keeping the skin on. Any other fish take the skin off. Squeeze lemon juice liberally on the fish. Dust steaks in seasoned flour. Heat the butter with capers. Sauté the fish on each side in the butter/capers until the fish is done. Be careful not to burn the butter. Remove the fish and add a little more flour to the butter. Stir to make a roux. Add 1/2 cup vermouth and cook down into a thin sauce. Cover half the serving plate with sauce on a warm plate. Place the fish on the sauce and garnish with greenery

www.ingramcontent.com/pod-product-compliance
Lightning Source LLC
Chambersburg PA
CBHW071438070526
44578CB00001B/130